UNDERSTANDING THE BOOKS OF THE OLD TESTAMENT

A GUIDE TO BIBLE STUDY FOR LAYMEN

Edited by

PATRICK H. CARMICHAEL

Prepared by

W. A. BENFIELD, Jr.   •   SAMUEL L. JOEKEL

PATRICK H. CARMICHAEL   •   E. D. KERR

KENNETH J. FOREMAN   •   JOHN C. SILER

JOHN KNOX PRESS   RICHMOND, VIRGINIA

Fourth printing 1970

Library of Congress Catalog Card Number: 61-9223

International Standard Book Number: 0-8042-3316-X

PREFACE
TO THE REVISED EDITION

The editor of the John Knox Press has given me the privilege of preparing such revisions of this volume as seem to be indicated by a careful reading of the material. I am proposing a few changes which I think will be helpful in the realization of the purpose set forth originally for the publication of such a work.

The principal changes occur in the section devoted to the major prophets where it is believed the reader will be greatly helped by breaking the material up into divisions in such a way that he can see at a glance the chief emphases. This should be helpful as he progresses in his reading and for purposes of review. The original content has not been materially changed.

A careful rereading of this material has given me a new appreciation of the original concept which guided the preparation of the manuscript, and for the splendid content which has been written into it by the several authors. So far as I know this is the only volume which offers the lay reader so much valuable guidance material for the self-study of the Old Testament. It is a resource which when used with the Bible, the Bible dictionary, and the commentary provides the earnest student unlimited assistance in his search for an understanding of the teachings of the Scriptures.

As the volume goes into its sixth printing, with revisions as indicated above, it is the sincere hope of the Editor that it will receive continued favor by students of the Bible and that its usefulness will be increased through the years.

Patrick H. Carmichael
Princeton, New Jersey

PREFACE

During more than a quarter of a century as professor of English Bible in college and theological seminary, Director of Leadership Education in the Presbyterian Church U. S., and chairman of the cycle graded subcommittee of the curriculum committee of the International Council of Religious Education, I have had a growing conviction that there should be a guide to Bible study written particularly for the lay man and woman. To meet this need I have asked men representing the pastorate, the college, the seminary, and church boards to join me in this enterprise.

We are presenting in this volume a series of six brief studies, each a complete unit in itself, which are so related as collectively to make a complete survey of the Old Testament. The writers were requested to limit their manuscripts to a maximum of ten thousand words. Obviously such a brief work cannot contain sufficient material to provide all the guidance in study that is needed. The writers were requested, therefore, to confine their references largely to three resource volumes: the *American Standard Version of the Bible, The Westminster Dictionary of the Bible,* and *The One Volume Bible Commentary* by Dummelow.* We recognize many other good dictionaries and commentaries which should be used freely by those who have access to them. Our purpose was to so limit reference material that individuals and groups might secure adequate resources in a comparatively small number of volumes and be assured of helps at hand for a long and continuous study of the Scriptures. Quotations from the American Standard Version are used by permission of the International Council of Religious Education.

We have endeavored to provide a comprehensive and constructive guide to individual study, for use in Bible classes in the Sunday school and elsewhere, as a basis for several courses in the Standard Leadership curriculum, as a rapid survey course for students in

---

* Readers of the revised edition of this book will want to use also the Revised Standard Version of the Bible.

schools and colleges and theological seminaries, and as refresher reading for the busy pastor who needs, from time to time, to take a fresh look at the contents of the Old Testament as a whole.

The contributors to this volume, listed in the order in which each one's material appears, are: John C. Siler, pastor of the Shepherdstown Presbyterian Church, Shepherdstown, West Virginia, and writer of uniform lesson helps for the *Earnest Worker;* Samuel L. Joekel, Professor of English Bible, Austin Presbyterian Theological Seminary; W. A. Benfield, Jr., pastor of the Highland Presbyterian Church, Louisville, Kentucky; Kenneth J. Foreman, Sr., Professor of Theology, Louisville Presbyterian Theological Seminary; E. D. Kerr, Professor of Old Testament, Columbia Theological Seminary; and Patrick H. Carmichael, Dean of the Faculty and Professor of Religious Education, the General Assembly's Training School for Lay Workers.

The work has been done in the full realization that the finished volume will contain a wide variety of guidance material because of two considerations: (1) the different sections of the Bible represent many types of literature which cannot best be interpreted by a uniform pattern; (2) six writers of such a work will obviously reflect their respective literary styles. Before submitting the manuscript for publication each writer was given an opportunity to read the whole, to revise his material if he wished to do so, and to make constructive suggestions for the revision of other sections. The volume therefore has had more than usual editorial study and revision.

I am greatly indebted to many friends, particularly to Mrs. Alma H. Clinevell, my efficient secretary for nine years, for her untiring service in preparing the original manuscript; to Miss Mary Virginia Robinson of John Knox Press for valuable suggestions in preparing the manuscript for publication; and to Mr. Robert A. Stratton, also of John Knox Press, for his interpretive illustrations.

Patrick H. Carmichael
Richmond, Virginia.

CONTENTS

OLD TESTAMENT SURVEY

JOHN C. SILER

OLD TESTAMENT SURVEY

OLD TESTAMENT SURVEY

I. Background of Universal History

Genesis 1:1—11:9

The Old Testament begins at the beginning by the introduction of God, who was already existent when all else began to exist. He is the eternal, self-existent, independent, personal power who moves in creation and directs the course of history. Genesis 1:1 is the key to the Old Testament, which from page to page unfolds the living and true God in his character and in his manifold working in the earth.

God is revealed as the Creator of all things. (1:2-31.) The universe is the product of divine energy (1:1), but the earth was not yet fit for the purpose of its Creator; it was chaos. The intelligent, loving, and gracious God now manifests his power in bringing order to the earth by the work of six creative days: (1) Light (3-5); (2) air and water (6-8); (3) land and plants (9-13); (4) lights (14-19); (5) fish and fowls (20-23); (6) animals (24-25) and man (26-31). The purpose of this great chapter is to impress upon us the fact of God as Creator. The matter of God's method in creation need not disturb us. The crowning creative act was man, a finite being endowed with God-like powers, involving intelligence, moral discernment, freedom of choice. To man the creature was given dominion over the earth, a grave responsibility.

On the seventh day God rested; his creative work in the earth was complete. (2:1-3.) Here we have the foundation upon which rests the observance of one day in seven as a period of rest.

God's thought for man as an intelligent, free being is revealed in Genesis 2:4-24. Man is placed in Eden to enjoy its benefits, with just one restriction, that he should not eat of the tree of the knowledge of good and evil. Man who had the power of choice must in justice be given the opportunity of choice if he is to become a moral being. Woman is created and marriage established in recognition of man as a social being.

13

All is not well with man as we know him. He no longer lives in Eden. The coming of sin into the world with its consequent suffering is told in a simple story (3:1-24), so true to life and experience. Temptation came to Eve, as to the rest of us, and under it both she and Adam made a wrong and disastrous choice. Adam and Eve became sinners, no longer finding delight in the companionship of God. We may condemn Eve for her act, but we consistently follow her example. We get our first glimpse of the terrible consequence of sin in the world in the slaying of Abel by Cain. (4:1-15.) Envy and hatred had gotten in their deadly work and are still at work.

In Genesis 4:16—5:32 are the two genealogical lines of Cain and of Seth, which have a bearing on the purpose of the Old Testament. In the line of Cain (4:16-24) we have the beginnings of material and cultural civilization. Cain himself built a city, marking the beginning of urban life. Jabel (vs. 20) began to develop agriculture and cattle-raising. Music began to be cultivated with Jubal (vs. 21), the forerunner of cultural progress. Tubal-cain was the father of industry (vs. 22), which has made such enormous progress in these modern times. Yet this material and cultural development found no higher expression than in Lamech's song in praise of the sword as an instrument of vengeance. (Vss. 23-24.) The narration of the line of Seth (4:25—5:32) seems to be a montonous recital of birth and death, but it has a distinctive spiritual quality, lacking in the line of Cain, for in this line men began to call upon the name of the Lord (4:26). In this line we have Enoch and Noah, and it continues on down the centuries to give to the world Abraham, David, Jesus. It is the line of spiritual power in the Old Testament. The line of Cain is pursued no further, because it is not the purpose of the Old Testament to narrate the material and cultural development of mankind.

Genesis 6:2 is a peculiar verse in which the sons of God are said to have married the daughters of men. Probably the best explanation is that the line of Seth and the line of Cain intermarried, with the result that the world was given over to material development and the loss of spiritual power. The world of that day turned from God to follow in its own way. (6:5-8.) The judgment of God falls upon man through the Flood, in which all mankind perished, save Noah and his family in the ark. (6:9—9:29.) That God will not permit evil to prevail in the earth is the lesson of the Flood.

After the Flood, mankind took a new start. The sons of Noah became heads of the three grand divisions of mankind: Semitic, Japhetic, and Hamitic peoples. Chapter 10 gives the early location of these people. The Hebrews were Semitic. But again mankind forgot to give God its loyal service and sought to defy him in the building of a tower so high as to reach to the very heavens. Again the judgment of God came upon them in the confounding of their speech (11:1-9), so that the people could no longer work together in the carrying out of their proud design. This is the biblical account of the origin of languages, and we are learning in this day that the presence in the world of so many different languages and dialects is a great hindrance to the working together of the peoples and races of the world. At Pentecost it was disclosed how this handicap might be overcome.

It is impossible to date the events of these chapters. It is not their purpose to record history as history, but to give an understanding of man—his origin, his nature, his progress, his failures—as a background for God's revelation and intervention for man's redemption.

II. THE TIMES OF THE PATRIARCHS

Genesis 11:10—15:26

Against the background of human failure and spiritual need the Old Testament begins to unfold the story of redemption. Its record now will be concerned with the origin and development of the Hebrew people, through whom the whole earth is to be blessed. (12:3.)

The period of the patriarchs was about 2000—1700 B.C. It seems to have been a time of important migrations among the peoples of the earth, one of which was the migration of the family of Terah from Ur to Haran, six hundred miles to the northwest. Abram was the son of Terah (11:27-32), whether the youngest or the oldest is hard to say. He married Sarai, his half-sister. It was this man who was destined under God to become the father of the Hebrew nation and whose name would be great in the earth. To Abram in Haran when he was seventy-five years old came the call to leave his kindred and to make his way to Canaan, four hundred miles to the southwest, under the promise of God to bless him and make him a blessing. (12:1-3.) This promise of God to Abram is the fountain from which flows the stream of Old Testament history. Abram took God at his word; "They went forth to go into the land of Canaan; and into the land of Canaan they came."

The record of Abraham's (Abram's) life in Canaan is preserved for us in Genesis 12:6—25:11. It was an eventful and prosperous life, characterized by loyalty and obedience to God. Abraham was indeed the friend of God, trusted, blessed, and honored by him. (See chs. 17—19.) The outstanding event in the life of Abraham was the birth of Isaac (21:1-8), along with the test of his faith in the offering of Isaac as a sacrifice (22:1-19). Another matter of the very greatest concern to Abraham was that Isaac should have a suitable wife. Here we have a contact with the family left behind in Padan-aram. (See the story in ch. 24.) Abraham died at the age of 175, having spent a hundred years in Canaan.

Isaac, the second of the patriarchs, was a quiet, retiring, affectionate man, whose life is summed up for us in Genesis 26. He is famed as being the digger of wells; but he was also the heir of the promise. (Heb. 11:9, 20.) Isaac spent his life in the south country of Canaan in the neighborhood of Beersheba, moving later on to Hebron, where he died at the age of 180. (35:27-29.)

Jacob, the third of the patriarchs, is one of the most familiar characters in Bible history. The story of his life begins at Genesis 25:19 and may be said to run through the remainder of the book. Jacob, like Abraham, was an epochal man. Jacob and Esau were twin sons of Isaac and Rebekah, with qualities so differing as to be outstanding. Jacob had little to commend him; even his name, Jacob, denoted deficiency in character. Having taken advantage of Esau in the matter of the birthright, and having brought the matter to a conclusion by deceiving his father into giving him the blessing of the first-born (25:27-34; 27:1—28:9), Jacob flees from Esau to Padan-aram to find refuge among his mother's kinspeople. In the course of twenty years much befalls Jacob (28:10—32:32), but his experiences at Bethel (28:10-22) and at Peniel (32:24-32) were unforgettable and transforming. Jacob stands out as a work of God's grace, which Jacob himself acknowledges. (48:15-16.) The event in the life of Jacob that had the most determining effect upon Hebrew history was his removal, with his family, from Canaan to Egypt (chs. 46—47), where he died at the age of 147, having lived 17 years in Egypt.

In reading the narrative of Jacob's family it is not hard to see that it was on the point of being absorbed into the life of Canaan. The life and work of Joseph in Egypt prevented this. The story of Joseph (chs. 37—45) is part of the life of Jacob, and should be studied as such. In Joseph, God was raising up a savior for Israel, to preserve them not only from famine, but also from the moral destruction that threatened. In Egypt the family of Jacob became a separated people. God uses men and nations for the accomplishment of his sovereign will.

III. ISRAEL DELIVERED FROM EGYPTIAN BONDAGE

Exodus—Deuteronomy

Joseph was sold into Egypt at a providential time. About 1720 B.C. Egypt was conquered by a people from Asia, who established themselves as rulers of the country. This is the period of the Shepherd kings (about 1720-1550 B.C.). These kings were intensely hated by the native Egyptians. It was not long after this foreign invasion that Joseph came into Egypt, and the presence of this alien government helps to account for his phenomenal rise to power. It was in this favorable period that Israel increased and multiplied in Goshen (Exod. 1:1-7) until they became a formidable host. About 1546 B.C. the Egyptians drove their foreign masters from power and established their own dynasty. When Israel had been in Egypt nearly four hundred years, Rameses II (about 1301-1234 B.C.) came to the throne. His long reign is noted for its building program. This is most probably the Pharaoh of the Oppression. He saw the danger of such a host of alien people in Egypt and instituted the policy of reducing them to slavery. (Exod. 1:8-22.)

In the early stages of Israel's oppression Moses was born and in the irony of providence was brought up under the Pharaoh whose heavy hand was upon Israel (Exod. 2), and was taught in all the learning of the Egyptians (Acts 7:21-22). The slaying of the Egyptian resulted in Moses' being forced to flee to Midian for safety, where he had another long period of training for his leadership in Israel. At last, after eighty years of training, the call came to him to deliver Israel from its bondage. (Exod. 3:1—6:8.)

The Pharaoh of the Exodus was probably Merneptah (about 1235-1227), son of Rameses II. (Though this chronology has its difficulties, it serves to provide chronological bearings for Old Testament study.) It was not easy for Pharaoh to let the Israelites leave Egypt, for they were an economic asset. God and Pharaoh struggled for the mastery for almost an entire year, during which ten plagues devastated Egypt (Exod. 7:1—13:16), the last one being the death of the first-born, from which Israel was saved by the sprinkling of the blood of the first Passover lamb. To commemorate the departure from Egypt the Passover was established to be observed by Israel perpetually. (Ch. 12.)

On leaving Egypt the Children of Israel made their way to the south, after crossing the Red Sea, until they came to Mount Sinai about 150 miles distant. Though Israel had escaped from the physical bondage of Egypt, it had yet a long way to go to escape its moral and spiritual bondage. Almost an entire year was spent at Sinai. Here they received the law of the Ten Commandments (Exod. 19:1—20:21) after entering into covenant relationship with God. In Sinai, Moses was given the statute laws of Israel recorded in Exodus 20:22—23:33, and also ceremonial laws. Here also Moses was instructed to build the Tabernacle after the pattern furnished, which was done, and the Tabernacle set up in the midst of the camp. (Exod. 25—40.) Another matter of large importance that appears to have been accomplished at this time was the organization of the people after the suggestion of Jethro, the father-in-law of Moses. (Exod. 18:13-27.) At Sinai, Israel received laws, a system of government, and a central place of worship.

A crucial situation arose at Kadesh-barnea, shortly after Israel left

Sinai. It was the intention of Moses to take possession of Canaan by entering from the south. With this in view he sent out the twelve spies to reconnoiter the land. The report of these spies regarding the strength of Canaan was so discouraging that the people refused to make an attempt at its conquest until too late. Only Joshua and Caleb saw the possibility under God of immediate possession. As a result of this refusal Israel was condemned to wander in the wilderness until all that cowardly and disloyal generation had died. The whole sad story is told in Numbers 13—14.

When the term of wilderness wanderings had expired we find Israel on the border of Moab, across the river Arnon. (Num. 20—21.) From this point the country east of the Jordan, (Trans-Jordan) was taken from Sihon king of the Amorites and from Og king of Bashan. (Num. 21:21-35.) From here they moved to Israel's last camping place before entering Canaan (Num. 22:1), a point east of the Jordan opposite Jericho. Events of great importance took place here. Moses in a solemn ceremony consecrated Joshua to succeed him as leader of Israel. (Num. 27:15-23.) The land conquered east of the Jordan was divided among the tribes of Reuben, Gad, and the half-tribe of Manasseh, on condition that they help the other tribes take possession of Canaan. (Num. 32.) It was here that Moses (Deut. 1:1) gave his wonderful review of Israel's history and laws, reported in Deuteronomy. It was from nearby Mount Nebo, on the summit of Mount Pisgah, that Moses saw stretched before him the magnificent view of Canaan, and there he died. (Deut. 34.)

IV. ISRAEL POSSESSES CANAAN

Joshua

In the forty years of wilderness life Israel has acquired a system of laws, an administrative government, and a mode of worship. The one need now is a land in which to establish themselves as a nation. The promise of Abraham included a land in which to dwell (Gen. 17:8), and now this promise is on the point of fulfillment.

The death of Moses brought Joshua into the position of leadership, having before him the definite task of subduing Canaan and dividing it among the tribes. Joshua is one of the strong characters in Hebrew history. He was a man of ability, courage, and strength, and above all he was a man of God. (Ch. 1.)

The first move was to bring the Children of Israel across the Jordan into Canaan. This host passed over Jordan on dry ground and set up camp at Gilgal, between the Jordan and Jericho. (Chs. 3—4.) The first thing Israel did in Canaan was to rededicate themselves to God and celebrate the Passover. (Ch. 5.) Israel's right to Canaan rested on their being the people of God.

Before Israel could occupy Canaan they must take possession of it. God did not hand them the land on a silver platter. Right at the very entrance to the land stood the strong walled city of Jericho, which must be taken before any progress could be made in the conquest of Canaan. The account of the fall of Jericho is a record of divine help (ch. 6), designed to give courage to Israel for the task before them. In the taking of Ai, near Bethel (chs. 7—8), Israel learned the wholesome lesson of obedience to God's will. The possession of Canaan was not to be an enterprise of personal aggrandizement.

The fall of Jericho and Ai, along with the abject surrender of the Gibeonites (ch. 9), forced an alliance of the five kings of southern Canaan for the purpose of chastising Gibeon. The Gibeonites called Joshua to their aid. Joshua defeated these five kings in the battle of Beth-horon. (10:1-27.) This defeat opened all of south Canaan to conquest, an opportunity which Joshua seized. (10:28-43.) One of the important things to note about this campaign is Joshua's failure to conquer the Philistines of the maritime plain. Had he done this the future of Israel might have been quite different.

When the news of the conquest of south Canaan came to Jabin, king of Hazor, he took immediate steps to form an alliance of all the small kingdoms of north Canaan against Joshua. Joshua accepted the challenge, defeated these kings at Lake Merom, and seized their kingdoms. (11:1-15.) In this way north Canaan fell to Israel. We have no account of the conquest of central Canaan, but from the book of Judges it appears that this was only a gradual process and that pockets of Canaanites remained here and there until the time of David.

Now that most of the land was in the possession of Israel, the next step was its division among the tribes. (Chs. 13—22.) Reuben, Gad, and one-half Manasseh had already received their portion in Gilead, east of Jordan. Southern Canaan was assigned to Simeon, Judah, Benjamin, and Dan. Dan later moved to the far north. (Judges 18.) Central Canaan fell to the lot of the house of Joseph— Ephraim and half the tribe of Manasseh. North Canaan was given to the tribes of Issachar, Zebulon, Asher, and Naphtali. Levi, the priestly tribe, was given possessions among the other twelve tribes.

The last two chapters of Joshua (23—24) reveal the anxiety of Joshua for the spiritual future of Israel. He saw the danger to the religious life of Israel that would likely come from the remnants of the Canaanite people still in the land, nor was he mistaken in this. Joshua sought to counteract this influence by securing from the people a pledge of loyalty to God, with his own decision to such loyalty as an example. Israel had followed him in the conquest of the land, they should now follow him in their devotion and loyalty to God.

This land that God gave Israel is one of the most remarkable small portions of earth to be found anywhere, and was peculiarly adapted to be the home of this people. This land of Israel, which we call Palestine (a name derived from the Philistines), is a small portion of the earth's surface, about the size of our state of Vermont, having an area of about 10,000 square miles. The Jordan divides it into two divisions: west of the Jordan is the Canaan of the Bible; east of the Jordan is Gilead. It falls into five physical divisions. Beginning on the west is the Maritime Plain, running the entire length of the country, save for the break at Mount Carmel. It was very fertile in Bible times. Next is the Low Country or Shephelah, which is composed of the foothills of the Central Range. Next is the Central Mountain Range that extends the whole length of Canaan until it runs out in the desert of the wanderings. Then there is that remarkable Jordan Valley, which begins at the foot of Mount Hermon 1,700 feet above sea level and descends to the Dead Sea 1,290 feet below the level of the sea. The fifth division is the fertile tableland east of the Jordan. These physical features gave to Palestine a variety of climate and a wide range of fruit and grain crops. There is a sense in which Palestine is an isolated country, lying as it does between the Mediterranean Sea and the Arabian Desert on the east and south; but in another sense it was far from isolated in Bible times. Canaan has been called "the Bridge," because it must be crossed in any communication, war or commerce, between the powers on the Euphrates and Tigris Rivers and Egypt on the Nile. The great caravan routes of antiquity passed through Palestine, bringing it into a position of importance in the commerce of the world, and making it bear the brunt of war between the nations on the Euphrates and Egypt on the Nile. A careful study of the geography and topography of Palestine will do much in helping us to understand the history of the Hebrew people.

V. THE PERIOD OF THE JUDGES

Judges
Ruth
I Samuel 1—8

Joshua's anxiety for the religious future of Israel was well-founded, as is shown by the book of Judges. "They [Israel] forsook the LORD, and served Baal and the Ashtaroth." (Judges 2:13.) The religion of the Canaanites had its appeal in the material and sensual satisfactions it offered. As fertility gods Baal and Ashtaroth offered prosperity to agricultural Israel. "Baal worship apparently had its origin in the belief that every tract of ground owed its productivity to a supernatural being, or *baal,* that dwelt there. The farmers probably thought that from the Baalim, or fertility gods, of various regions came the increase of crops, fruit, and cattle." Ashtaroth was the female divinity. "She was the goddess of sexual love, maternity, and fertility. Prostitution as a religious rite in the service of this goddess under various names is widely attested." (Westminster Bible dictionary.) The student of the Old Testament needs to grasp the significance of idolatry as the exaltation of the material and the sensual to the place of supremacy in life. The worship of Jehovah and obedience to his commandments was in direct opposition to all this. The book of Judges records a struggle between God and the world that is still going on.

The length of time covered by the book of Judges is one of the difficulties of Bible chronology. By adding together the length of time mentioned in the book we have a sum of more than four hundred years, which is quite too long. It is probable that some of these judges were contemporary, which could shorten the period considerably. We will have to wait for more light before we can have an assured chronology.

In the book of Judges we have twelve judges, six of them accounted for in some detail, the other six barely mentioned. In addition there is an account of the upstart king Abimelech. These judges were not officials in the usual sense of the term, but were liberators of the people from some severe oppression that had fallen upon them from neighboring peoples. The first judge was Othniel. (3:7-11.) Ehud delievered Israel from Moab. (3: 12-30.) Deborah, the famous woman judge, was instrumental in bringing deliverance to north Israel from a northern alliance. (Chs. 4—5.) One of the worst experiences that befell Israel was the inroads of the plundering Midianites from which they were set free by Gideon. (Chs. 6—8.) Gideon's son, Abimelech, attempted to establish a kingdom at Shechem, but failed. (Ch. 9.) Jephthah is another notable judge who delivered Israel from the marauding Ammonites. (Chs. 10—12.) The exploits of Samson against the Philistines are narrated in detail. (Chs. 13—16.) The remaining chapters of Judges give us an insight into the crudity and confusion of the period.

The book of Ruth belongs to the times of the Judges, showing that beauty, goodness, loyalty, and faith still existed in those difficult times.

The first eight chapters of I Samuel depict one of the very critical situations in Hebrew history. The worship of Jehovah was at its lowest ebb. (2:12-36.) Eli had combined the offices of priest and judge, with the seat of government at Shiloh, where the Tabernacle had been set up. He had grown old in years and had become negligent of his official duties. His sons were using their priestly office as an opportunity for graft and extortion.

The Philistines were the oppressors of Israel (Judges 13:1), and in the first battle of Ebenezer (I Sam. 4) defeated Israel and carried away the Ark into their own land. Archeology seems to bear testimony to the destruction of Shiloh at this time. We know that it was no longer the center of worship. The loss of the Ark was a serious blow, indicating that God had departed from Israel. The adverse experiences of the Philistines with the Ark (ch. 5) led them to return it to Israel (ch. 6), where it was placed in the house of Abinidab (7:1-2). It would appear from this that the religious structure of Israel was in great confusion. This was indeed a dark time.

It was in those days that Samuel the prophet and last judge did his great work in Israel in keeping true religion alive and doing much to keep the Philistines at bay. Samuel's importance in Hebrew history is greater than we might ordinarily suspect from the brevity of the record, but when viewed from the background of Israel's situation, his greatness is manifest. We are told of his childhood and call in chapters 1 and 3 of I Samuel. His development was such that all Israel knew that Samuel was a prophet of Jehovah. (3:20.) His effective spiritual ministry came to a climax at Mizpah in Israel's repentance and acknowledgment of God. (7:3-6.) In the second battle of Ebenezer the Philistines met defeat, which resulted in the establishment of peace. (7:7-14.) The summary of Samuel's ministry as judge and acting priest is given in 7:15-17. See 12:1-5 for Samuel's record as administrator in Israel.

It was given to Samuel to become the founder of Israel's government under kings. Chapter 8 tells the story of how this change in government came about. Samuel anointed both Saul (chs. 9—10) and David (ch. 16) to be kings over Israel.

VI. THE UNITED KINGDOM: THE PERIOD OF ISRAEL'S GLORY

I Samuel 9—31
II Samuel
I Kings 1—11
I Chronicles 10—29
II Chronicles 1—9

In this period of Israel's history three personalities stand out— Saul, David, Solomon—each one making his own contribution to history and to life.

Saul the son of Kish of the small tribe of Benjamin became Israel's first king. (I Sam. 9—31.) It is conjectured that he was about thirty-five when he came to the throne. The Old Testament does not give the length of his reign, but Paul says it was forty years. (Acts 13:21.) Saul's great contribution to our history was the welding of the tribes of Israel under a central government, thus preparing the way for David. He did succeed in overcoming the Philistines and other enemies of Israel at least temporarily, thus giving Israel opportunity for national development. The reign of Saul was spoiled by his acts of disobedience, which brought about his consequent rejection. He was both friend and enemy of the young David, who learned at Saul's court much that was helpful for his future as king of Israel.

David is the great name in Hebrew history. We are told more about him than any other character in the Old Testament. He was a versatile man, being warrior, statesman, administrator, musician, poet. We will follow his record as given in II Samuel. David was thirty years old when he became king, and he reigned for forty years. (II Sam. 5:4.) The date for his reign is about 1010-970 B.C. His reign falls into two sections, 7½ years over Judah with Hebron as his capital, and 33 years over all Israel, with the capital at Jerusalem. (5:5.) Despite his faults David was a great and good king, aptly summarized in the words, "David executed justice and righteousness unto all his people." (8:15.) David accomplished some very important things for Israel. (1) He subdued all the surrounding enemies of Israel. (Ch. 8.) He so completely subdued the Philistines that they never recovered their former power. He brought Moab and Edom under subjection, and extended his power to the north in bringing Damascus under tribute. (2) David extended the territory of Israel to its promised limits as given in Joshua 1:4. (3) David made Jerusalem the capital of his kingdom. (5:6-10.) This was a master stroke of statesmanship, because Jerusalem was ideally located both physically and politically for such a position in the state. It was protected by its surrounding hills, and was a city of the smallest tribe of Benjamin. (4) David gave Israel an organized and efficient government. (8:15-18.) (5) David gave distinct recognition to God in his kingdom. (Chs. 6—7.) This was David's outstanding contribution to the world as a statesman. He saw that religion was an essential in the maintenance of national unity and for the moral life of the people. To these ends he brought the Ark into Jerusalem and set it in the very midst of his kingdom as the symbol of God's presence. When Israel was freed from its enemies and the kingdom firmly established (7:1), David turned his thoughts toward the building of a temple that would do honor to Israel's God. While it was not permitted to David to be the builder of the Temple, the assurance that his throne would be established forever was given him. (7:16.) David was the great kingly ancestor of Jesus Christ, the Messianic King who upholds forever David's reign of righteousness and justice.

Solomon was but a boy, probably about eighteen, when he succeeded to the throne. His mother was Bathsheba. Solomon reigned over Israel forty years (970-930 B.C.). (I Kings 11:42.) In these years the kingdom of Israel became rich and magnificent through its varied industries and commerce, the record of which is found in I Kings 1—11. (1) Solomon gave impetus to commerce. Up to this time Israel had given little thought to commercial ventures. Solomon's treaty with Hiram of Tyre (5:1-12) gave him a connection with the most important commercial kingdom of the time and access to abundant resources of exchange for goods. He also built a fleet of ships that carried the commerce of Israel afar. (9:26-28.) The result of Solomon's adventure into commerce was to make silver as abundant as stone in Jerusalem. (10:27.) (2) Solomon was a great builder. (9:15-19.) His most remarkable structure was the Temple. (Ch. 6.) He built a magnificent palace for himself. (Ch. 7.) He fortified Jerusalem and built cities, all of which bespeak an immense prosperity. (Ch. 9.) (3) Solomon gave Israel an efficient organization. (Ch. 4.) He divided the kingdom into twelve districts, each having its own officer who was charged with the responsibility of providing food for the king's household one month in the year. In 4:22-23 we are given some idea of the amount of provisions required. Solomon's Oriental magnificence placed a heavy tax burden on the people. (4) Solomon sought to bind his kingdom to the surrounding kingdoms by marriage alliances (3:1), which largely accounts for his large harem (11:1-8). This practice introduced alien religions into the heart of the kingdom and laid an immense burden of luxury on the backs of the people. Solomon in all his glory was a magnificent Oriental monarch, but the forced labor and the excessive taxation required to support this splendor wrought grave dissatisfaction among the northern tribes who were bearing the brunt, bringing about the rebellion of Jeroboam (11:26-40) and the division of the kingdom. In these three reigns (about one hundred years) Israel rose from the rustic simplicity of Saul's court to the splendor of Solomon, only to become a broken kingdom in the end. The trouble did not come out of the simplicity of Saul or the piety of David, but out of the wealth, magnificence, and luxury of Solomon, who forgot the common people in his own exaltation.

VII. THE NORTHERN KINGDOM

I Kings 12:1—22:53
II Kings 1:1—17:41

When Rehoboam, the son of Solomon, came to the throne (about 930 B.C.) the discontent within Israel came to a crisis, resulting in the division of the kingdom. This might have been prevented had Rehoboam been wise in making concessions (I Kings 12), although the jealousy between the Joseph tribes (Ephraim and Manasseh) and Judah seems to have been of long standing. A similar division took place at the beginning of David's reign. (II Sam. 2:8-11.) The northern tribes had a strong leader in Jeroboam, whom Solomon had placed over his forced labor. (I Kings 11:28.) Jeroboam was made king over Israel (northern tribes) (I Kings 12:20), while Rehoboam continued the line of David in Judah (Southern Kingdom).

The Northern Kingdom had every material advantage over Judah, being greater in area, fertility, and population. Judah was poor and desolate in comparison. The Northern Kingdom lasted about two hundred years (930-722 B.C.), in which time it had nineteen kings and nine dynasties. Eight of its kings met death by violence, and all of them were bad kings from the standpoint of religion. Not one made an attempt to establish the true worship of Jehovah. The tragedy of this kingdom was its utter destruction—no remnant being left, as in the Southern Kingdom, to rebuild or to keep alive its traditions.

Jeroboam I set the pattern for the religion of Israel by debasing the worship of Jehovah under the symbol of a calf. Two calf-shrines were erected, one at Bethel, the other at Dan, as the centers of worship, the political purpose being to keep the people of Israel from going to Jerusalem to worship in the Temple. Bethel became the renowned center for worship in Israel, with a worship very formal and elaborate, meriting the condemnation of Amos and Hosea. Through the narrative of the Northern Kingdom runs the refrain, "walked in the way of Jeroboam." (I Kings 12:25—16:14.)

About 885 B.C. a military leader by the name of Omri (I Kings 16:15-28) made himself king over Israel. He was evidently a king of considerable power, for the Assyrian records of this period mention "the house of Omri." About this time Syria to the north of Israel (Damascus its capital) became an active enemy of Israel, and the world power Assyria began to be a factor in Bible history. Omri built Samaria and made it the capital of the kingdom of Israel.

Omri was succeeded by his son Ahab (I Kings 16:29—22:40), who, through his wife Jezebel, introduced the Baal worship of Sidon into Israel. Baal with its female divinity Astarte was a fertility religion that practiced licentious and degrading forms of worship. Israel fell to the temptation of prosperity and pleasure. It was at this critical juncture that Elijah and Elisha appeared to combat this great evil. It is the work of these great prophets that fills the Bible narrative at this crucial point. Ahab was succeeded by two of his sons, Ahaziah and Jehoram (Joram). (I Kings 22:51—II Kings 8:29.)

The anointing of Jehu to be king over Israel (II Kings 9) began a dynasty that lasted almost a hundred years (842-745 B.C.). The important work of Jehu was the obliteration of Baal worship from Israel, and for this the Lord promised him a dynasty to the fourth generation. (II Kings 10:30.) Jehu did not establish the true worship of Jehovah, but continued in the way of Jeroboam I. (Vs. 31.) During the reigns of Jehu and his son Jehoahaz, Syria had succeeded in bringing Israel very low. (II Kings 10:32-33; 13:22.) Things took a turn for the better in the reign of Joash (Jehoash). (13:25.) It was in the long reign of Jeroboam II (41 years) that the Northern Kingdom attained its greatest power and glory. (II Kings 14:23-29.) Jonah the prophet had a part in this. At this time Assyria was having its own troubles in the east, which gave Jeroboam his opportunity to overcome weakened Syria. Amos and Hosea pointed out the superficial nature of this prosperity and warned Israel that it could not last. This marks the beginning of the great writing prophets, Amos about 760-746 B.C., Hosea probably 760-720 B.C. A study of these two prophets is the best source for the understanding of the last days of the Northern Kingdom.

Second Kings, chapters 15 and 17, tells the sad story of the disintegration of the Northern Kingdom, the fall of Samaria, and the disappearance of the ten northern tribes of Israel from history. In a period of less than twenty-five years (745-722 B.C.) the prosperity of Jeroboam II turned into confusion, anarchy, violence, ruin, and captivity. Zechariah, the fourth generation from Jehu, succeeded to the throne, but lasted only six months. Shallum was displaced by the cruel Menahem (15:14) after a reign of one month. Assyria had now regained her power and was pushing her conquests in the West. Menahem had to buy his kingdom from Pul of Assyria and squeezed Israel for the money. (15:19-20.) His son Pekahiah had an insignificant reign of two years until assassinated by Pekah. Hosea seems to be describing these times: "They are all hot as an oven, and devour their judges; all their kings are fallen: there is none among them that calleth unto me." (Hosea 7:7.) Pekah reigned twenty years, during which he formed an alliance with Syria for the invasion of Judah for the purpose of forcing Ahaz into a western alliance to check the advance of Assyria. (Isa. 7.) The attempt was to no avail, for Tiglath-pileser made serious inroads and carried some of the people of Israel captive to Assyria. (II Kings 15:29-31.) Hoshea was the last king of Israel. (II Kings 17:1-6.) He was evidently placed on the throne by Assyria, but sought to escape the payment of tribute by entering into an alliance with Egypt against Assyria. This brought Shalmaneser into the land in power with the determination to overthrow the kingdom. Samaria was besieged and the king imprisoned. Shalmaneser did not live to complete the conquest, but his successor, Sargon, completed it in 722 B.C. by the capture of Samaria and the dispersion of the people. The reason God permitted all this to befall Israel is given in II Kings 17:7-18.

VIII. THE SOUTHERN KINGDOM

I Kings 12:1—22:53
II Kings 1:1—25:30
II Chronicles 10:1—36:21

The Southern Kingdom was composed of the tribes of Judah and Benjamin, who remained loyal to Rehoboam. (II Kings 12:20-21.) Judah was by far the larger and more important tribe and for this reason the Southern Kingdom is known as Judah. It occupied southern Canaan and was mostly hill country, running into desert in the extreme south. Its chief wealth consisted in livestock, the land being good for grazing but poor for agriculture. This kingdom lasted more than a hundred and thirty years longer than the Northern (930-586 B.C.) and had the same number of kings, nineteen, not counting Athaliah, all of whom were of David's line. Seven of these kings are accounted good: Asa, Jehoshaphat, Amaziah, Uzziah, Jotham, Hezekiah, Josiah; the last two named appear as the best of the seven. The Southern Kingdom had the advantage of being set off from the world powers in its location, in its having the Northern Kingdom as a buffer state, and in its poverty. Judah fell not because it was an attractive field for conquest, but because of its political entanglements and duplicity.

Rehoboam was the first king of the Southern Kingdom as such. It was his folly that brought about the division. (I Kings 12:12-20.) The tragedy of this reign was the invasion of Shishak of Egypt who looted the kingdom. (I Kings 14:25-26.) Under the long reigns of two good kings, Asa and Jehoshaphat, Judah enjoyed much prosperity. (I Kings 15:9-24; 22:41-50.) Over a period of sixty years the Northern and Southern Kingdoms were at war with each other until peace was established between Ahab and Jehoshaphat. (See ch. 22.)

The peace between Jehoshaphat and Ahab brought a serious religious and political crisis in the Southern Kingdom. The story is told in II Kings 11. Some years before the events of chapter 11 Jehoram, the son of the good Jehoshaphat, married Athaliah, the daughter of Ahab and Jezebel. (II Kings 8:16-19.) Athaliah was a strong and determined woman like her mother. She brought her Baal worship with her into Judah and trained her son Ahaziah (also referred to as Jehoahaz and as Azariah) in it. This son was slain by Jehu after a reign of one year. (II Kings 8:25-29; 9:27-28.) Athaliah then took over the government and slayed her own grandchildren, only the baby Joash escaping. It was her design to exterminate the house of David, which for a time depended upon the safety of a baby boy. Athaliah reigned about six years, being the only reigning queen in either kingdom, and the one break in the line of David in Judah. In the reigns of Joash (Jehoash) and Amaziah, Baal worship was eradicated from Judah, though much idolatry was permitted to remain. (II Kings 12—14.)

The period in Judah's history that begins with Uzziah or Azariah (II Kings 14:21) and ends with Hezekiah (20:21) was the era of Isaiah (1:1) and his contemporary Micah (1:1). A reading of Isaiah 1—39 and the book of Micah gives the best insight possible into these times. Uzziah was the contemporary of Jeroboam II and shared in his prosperity. But by the time Ahaz (736-721 B.C.) came into power, events of world import began to take place. (II Kings 16.) The Northern Kingdom was declining, Assyria was beginning its westward march and was pressing hard on Syria. Pekah of Israel and Rezin of Syria invaded Judah to force Ahaz into an alliance with them to check the advance of Assyria. Ahaz, contrary to the advice of Isaiah (Isa. 7), secured the help of Tiglath-pileser of Assyria by paying a considerable price. Hezekiah, one of the best of Judah's kings, succeeded Ahaz. (II Kings 18:1-7.) In the sixth year of his reign the Northern Kingdom fell to the Assyrians, thus opening the way for the invasion of Judah a few years later by Sennacherib. (18:13 ff.) The first appearance of Babylon in the history of the Southern Kingdom is an innocent appearing circumstance (20:

12-19), but Isaiah saw its meaning for the future. With Assyria as a constant menace to the security of the Southern Kingdom, there arose the policy of foreign alliances, especially with Egypt, which Isaiah strongly opposed.

Manasseh succeeded his father Hezekiah, and to him it was given to have the longest (55 years) and the wickedest reign in the annals of Judah (21:1-9), and the two-year reign of his son Amon was no improvement (21:19-26). But these two wicked kings were succeeded by Josiah (22:1—23:30), who was outstanding in his zeal for God. This was the beginning of the time of Jeremiah (Jer. 1:1-3), and it may be that the young Jeremiah had much to do with the reforms of Josiah. Josiah came to a tragic death on the field of battle at the age of thirty-nine while seeking to prevent Pharaoh Neco of Egypt from passing through Palestine on his way to make war on Assyria. (23:29.) Pharaoh Neco continued his march, not knowing that the power of Assyria had succumbed to the might of Babylon; consequently he met the Babylonians under Nebuchadnezzar at Carchemish (605 B.C.) and was defeated. This defeat made Babylon the supreme world power. We can see the wisdom of Jeremiah's counsel of submission.

The remaining years of the Southern Kingdom were years of sorrow. Through the words of Jeremiah we sense the gravity of the times. After the death of Josiah the people made his son Jehoahaz (Shallum) king, but after an evil reign of three months he was deposed by Pharaoh and his brother Eliakim (name changed to Jehoiakim) was set on the throne. (II Kings 23:31-37.) Nebuchadnezzar lost no time in dealing with this vassal of Egypt, but after three years he rebelled and brought the power of Babylon upon himself and the kingdom. (24:1-7.) His son and successor, Jehoiachin (Jeconiah, Coniah), after a reign of three months was carried away to Babylon, along with the best people and much treasure. (24:8-17.) This was in 597 B.C. Nebuchadnezzar placed Zedekiah (Mattaniah) on the throne, which he held for eleven years as a subject of Babylon; but for some reason he rebelled and brought on the final blow. Zedekiah's eyes were put out and he was taken captive to Babylon. The city of Jerusalem was laid waste and the Temple destroyed. The treasure of

Temple and kingdom was seized, and almost the entire population was carried to Babylon as captives. The year 586 B.C. was a tragic one for the Southern Kingdom. The few poor people left behind to care for the land, with Gedaliah as their governor, soon fell on evil times. Gedaliah was slain, and for fear of the Babylonians the people fled to Egypt. (25:1-26.)

IX. EXILE AND RESTORATION

II Chronicles 36:20-23
Ezra
Nehemiah
Esther

The captive Jews in Babylon found themselves in a situation very different from their life in Canaan. They were victims of war in a strange land. We have very little information concerning these years of exile. Ezekiel, one of the 597 B.C. captives, lived and prophesied among them. His first task was to make it clear that there was no hope for restoration for some time to come and that they should become adjusted to their new country and life. After the news had been received that Jerusalem was destroyed (Ezek. 33:21-22), Ezekiel began to look to the future of Israel. Jeremiah wrote a letter to the exiles (Jer. 29:1-14) in which he advised them to build houses, to plant gardens in Babylon, and to enter upon a settled life, at the same time assuring them of release at the end of seventy years. A large number of these Jews took this advice to the extent of becoming so content with their surroundings as to make Babylon their permanent home. But there was a group of devout Jews who had a great longing for Canaan and for the worship of the Temple. (Ps. 137.)

Near the close of the period of captivity a new world power came upon the scene, Cyrus the Persian conquered Babylon in 539 B.C. and made himself ruler. One of the first acts of Cyrus was to issue a decree giving the Jews permission to return to Canaan and to re-build the Temple. (Ezra 1:1-4.) This decree set the stream of Hebrew history flowing freely again. Immediately about fifty thousand persons (round number) under Zerubbabel as governor and Joshua (Jeshua) as high priest left Babylon for Canaan. Soon after their arrival in Jerusalem (538 B.C.) they rebuilt the altar and restored sacrificial worship, and in the second year they laid the foundations of the Temple. The building of the Temple was interrupted until 520 B.C., when the prophets Haggai and Zechariah stirred up the people to complete the work. The second Temple was completed in the early spring of 515 B.C.

Probably about sixty years intervened between the completion of the Temple and the mission of Ezra. In this time the returned exiles had settled into a quiet life, intermarrying with those who had taken possession of the country in their absence, and gradually becoming lax in their religious observances. Ezra's purpose in going to Jerusalem was to teach the law of God, to beautify the Temple, and to restore its services. He was accompanied by about 1,755 men, many of them priests and Temple singers. It took four months to reach his destination, which was probably in the seventh year of Artaxerxes I, 458-457 B.C. Ezra was sorely troubled by the spiritual situation he found. (Ezra 7—10.)

Nehemiah is thought to have arrived in Jerusalem thirteen years after Ezra, 444 B.C. The Jews had been back in the ruined city of Jerusalem nearly a hundred years, but in that time they had done little toward rebuilding the city and its walls. When Nehemiah heard of this state of Jerusalem he was sorely troubled. Artaxerxes, discovering the reason for the sadness of his favorite official (cupbearer), gave him permission to go to Jerusalem to superintend the rebuilding of its walls on condition that he return when the task was completed. (Neh. 1:1—2:8.) The story of the rebuilding of the walls of Jerusalem in the space of fifty-two days is told in Nehemiah 2:9—6:19. From this point on we find Ezra and Nehemiah working together to bring the Jews in Palestine to a better understanding and observance of the law.

Judaism had its beginnings in this period. The Law came to have a place of high authority, as it should, but with it came those burdensome rules that destroyed its spirit. Many scholars attribute to

Ezra the formation of the Old Testament, practically as we have it now. Jewish tradition makes Ezra the writer of I and II Chronicles.

X. FROM MALACHI TO MATTHEW

The so-called "four silent centuries" that intervene between the close of the Old Testament and the beginning of the New Testament are full of interest for the Bible student. They have been called "the bridge between the Testaments." Dr. Henry Kendall Booth gives this description of these centuries: "These four forgotten centuries are replete with stirring events, heroic achievements, picturesque personalities, significant movements, and vocal with vivid narratives, charming stories, great sayings, and noble dreams. God was still at work within Israel preparing for the advent of His Son. To know this era is vital to the understanding of Jesus and His times." (*The Bridge Between the Testaments.*) Dummelow's one-volume commentary contains an excellent article on the history and literature of these centuries.

At the close of Malachi, Persia was the dominating world power, and continued so for another century, though we know little of her relation to the Jews in Palestine. The Persian period covered the era from 539-334 B.C.

Alexander the Great subjugated the Persian Empire. His conquering armies in their eastward sweep (334-323 B.C.) brought all western Asia under his control. Jerusalem came into his possession without a struggle. In 332 B.C. Alexander founded the city of Alexandria, which became a center of Greek learning and culture, and the home of a large colony of Jews. The conquests of Alexander the Great spread the Greek language through western Asia and caused Greek thought and ideals to permeate the thought of the people. This dissemination of the Greek language and culture made way for the translation of the Old Testament into Greek (the Septuagint), which in time became the Bible of the Greek-speaking Jews. The New Testament was written in Greek, and it was the language Paul used in preaching the gospel to the western world.

At the death of Alexander (323 B.C.), his kingdom was divided among his generals; Egypt under the Ptolemies and Syria under the

Seleucids concerned the destiny of the Jews in Palestine. It is not surprising that Palestine, by reason of its location between the two, should become a bone of contention. However, in 320 B.C. it came under the rule of Egypt where it remained until 198 B.C. In this period the Jews in Palestine prospered and were given a large measure of religious freedom, but they were gradually coming under the power of Greek (Hellenistic) influence. At the end of this period Syria succeeded in wresting Palestine from Egypt under Antiochus the Great (223-187 B.C.). Syria (Antioch its capital) was a stronger Hellenizing influence than Egypt. It was Antiochus Epiphanes (175-163 B.C.) who brought matters to the point of conflict. He determined to bring the Jews into line with Greek thought and ideals. He treated the orthodox party (Pharisees of N.T.) with merciless severity. He entered the Temple and robbed it of its sacred vessels. He recast the service after the forms of the Greek religion. Worst of all, he set up an image of Zeus within the Temple. The Hebrew religion was never in greater peril than now.

This harsh and drastic attempt to destroy the Jewish religion brought about one of the most heroic and sublime periods in Hebrew history. Every Christian should read the First Book of Maccabees. Mattathias, an old country priest, could not stand the sight of a Jew offering a heathen sacrifice and slew him, along with a Syrian officer who was enforcing these laws. Fleeing into the wilderness with his five sons, Mattathias gathered others about him and raised the standard of revolt. On his death in 166 B.C., his son Judas, known as Maccabaeus, or "the hammer," took over the leadership, and in two years won such remarkable victories as to clear the land of the Syrians, save for the Jerusalem garrison. On December 25, 165 B.C., the Temple was rededicated and its worship restored. In commemoration of this, the Feast of Dedication was appointed. (John 10:22.) Judas Maccabaeus continued the struggle, now for political freedom, which was gained under Simon the Maccabee about 142 B.C. The next eighty years of Jewish history were so full of internal strife and rivalry as to make the most unpleasant reading. The strife rose to such a pitch that the Roman general Pompey, then at Damascus, was invited in to take charge of affairs.

Pompey lost no time in marching upon Jerusalem, which he took in 63 B.C. The Jews lost their independence and came under Roman dominion. In 37 B.C. the Idumean Herod, by the authority of Rome, became the ruler of Palestine, and continued to reign until his death in 4 B.C., shortly after the birth of Jesus. He was an unscrupulous and cruel monarch, a lover of power, and guilty of political intrigue. His greatest work was the rebuilding of the Temple, which was begun in 20 B.C. and was not yet completed in the time of our Lord. (John 2:20.)

THE PENTATEUCH

GENESIS through DEUTERONOMY

SAMUEL L. JOEKEL

THE PENTATEUCH

GENESIS: THE GENERATIONS OF THE REDEMPTIVE NATION

> I. God's Redemptive Purpose Traced from Adam to Abraham. Genesis 1—11.
>
> II. God's Redemptive Purpose Traced from Abraham to Joseph. Genesis 12—50.

EXODUS: THE EMERGENCE OF THE REDEMPTIVE NATION; THE INSTITUTIONS AND THE CONSTITUTION OF ISRAEL

> I. The Deliverance from Bondage; The Passover. Exodus 1—15.
>
> II. The Hebrew State; The Law. Exodus 16—24.
>
> III. God's Dwelling Place: The Tabernacle. Exodus 25—40.

LEVITICUS: ACCESS TO GOD

> I. Access to God Attained Through Atonement. Leviticus 1—17.
>
> II. Access to God Maintained Through Holiness. Leviticus 18—27.

NUMBERS: THE DISCIPLINE OF THE REDEMPTIVE NATION

> I. The Journey Toward the Goal. Numbers 1:1—20:13.
>
> II. The Goal in Sight; Preparation for the Conquest of Canaan. Numbers 20:14—36:13.

DEUTERONOMY: THE REPETITION OF THE LAW

> The Age and Authorship of Deuteronomy; The Three Farewell Addresses of Moses. Deuteronomy 1—34.

THE PENTATEUCH

INTRODUCTION

The Age and Authorship of the Pentateuch

The first five books of the Bible bear no titles in the original Hebrew. They were designated by the ancient scribes by memorizing the first few words of the opening sentence of each. They comprise a definite section of the Old Testament, called in Hebrew the Law or "Torah," and in later Greek, the Pentateuch—literally, "The five-fold book."

Hebrew tradition makes Moses the author of all five, and the New Testament quotes from them frequently as his work. The traditional date of Moses is about 1290 B.C. In several places in the Pentateuch, Moses is spoken of as having recorded the events described, or as having been directed to record them. See Exodus 17:14; Exodus 20—24; 34:10-28; and also Deuteronomy 31 and 32. All the books of Pentateuch were originally anonymous, and Moses nowhere claims to be the author of the whole. The captions in the King James Version are obviously the work of revisers.

Over against this traditional view is the documentary hypothesis which declares that the Pentateuch is a compilation of documents by some priestly redactor or editor, sometimes designated as R. Several attempts at a critical and scientific study of the Pentateuch were made as early as the seventeenth century, but chief credit goes to Jean Astruc, physician to Louis the XIV (1753) for the first systematic study. It is based on the supposed discovery of different documents and codes, which, it is contended, were written at various times by different scribes and priests. These writers or compilers are identified by their consistent use of certain names for God. One who uses only the name God (Elohim) as in Genesis 20:1-18 and in 22:1-13 is designated E. Another uses only the word LORD (Jehovah) as in Genesis 4. He is called J. Each of these sections is a complete story in itself. Where these two stories are woven together by a later editor the initials JE are used. There is also the section called C (the Covenant) in Exodus 20—24; the Priestly documents called P, P′, etc., in Leviticus; the Holiness or Separation code in Leviticus 18—20; and D, which makes up most of the book of Deuteronomy. This view would make the Redactor to be a prophet or a priestly writer who lived at least as late as the times of the kings and prophets in the seventh century B.C. For a fuller explanation of this problem, the student should read the introduction to the Pentateuch in Dummelow's one-volume commentary, or Raven, *The Introduction to the Old Testament.*

GENESIS

The Generations of the Redemptive Nation

The first book in the Pentateuch was originally designated by the Hebrew word for its first phrase, "in-the-beginning" (*B'reshith*). The Greek word "Genesis" means "beginning." Its date and authorship have already been discussed.

The purpose of the book of Genesis is *religious*. When this is understood the so-called conflict between Genesis and science will be done away. It was never meant to be a textbook on geology, geography, history, or anthropology. Its purpose is to show, by selected narratives, the hand of God in human history up to the time of his selecting and drawing out one nation to be his redemptive agent. If we draw a triangle, wide at the base with converging lines narrowing as they reach the top, calling the base line "Adam" or "the race," then narrowing up successively to Noah and his sons; Shem; Terah; Abraham; Isaac; and finally, Jacob, or Israel—God's redemptive agent—we shall have a diagram or scheme of the book.

As to divisions, there is an introductory Poem of Creation, followed by ten sections, each introduced by the phrase, "these are the generations," from which the book gets its name. Our following study will resolve the book into two main sections.

I. GOD'S REDEMPTIVE PURPOSE TRACED FROM ADAM TO ABRAHAM

Genesis 1:1—11:26

The Poem of Creation. (1:1—2:4a.) Here we have seven stanzas, six of which close with the refrain, "there was evening and there was morning." The order of creation follows that of science: first, light and darkness; then the heavens and the water; then the earth and plant life; next the solar system, dividing time into days, seasons, years; then the fishes and fowls; and lastly, on the sixth day, land animals and man.

Man is a separate creation, created as God's climax, not like the other creatures "after their kind," but "in the image of God." He is the spiritual creation; the soul-bearer; the child of God, with capacity for religion—an endowment reserved for him alone. This is the great unbridgeable gap between man and the animal creation.

The significance of this poem is to teach that creation is the work of God, who used successive steps, in an orderly process, climaxing in the creation of man made in the image of God. The poem closes with the institution of the Sabbath set apart and hallowed by the Lord himself. Two primal institutions are thus noted in this opening section: the family as the basic unit of society in 1:27, and the Sabbath in 2:2-3.

The Generations of the Heavens and the Earth. (2:4b—4:26.) This second story of the creation, in prose, centers about man—created by God perfect, a living soul, surrounded by Paradise or Eden. To complete the picture, woman was created to be a companion and helper for man. Note again the foundation for the first institution—the home—and the one-man-one-woman ideal for marriage.

Chapter 3 is pivotal. It is called the fall of man. It holds the basic theological teachings of the Bible. It is the plot of the whole Book. It is the story of the nature and effect of sin, the separator between God and man, and brings to us the promise of the way back to God. The chief characters in the story of God and man are portrayed. God and man are *at-one* as the story opens. Sin has an author, the Adversary, or Satan. God is not the author of sin. The Adversary works by a permissive decree of God. (See Job, chs. 1—2.) The serpent tempted our first parents by questioning the validity of their trust and confidence in God, which resulted in outright disobedience. Sin in its nature also affects others. Eve gave to Adam and he did eat.

The effect of sin was immediately evident. The "at-one-ment" of God and man was destroyed. Sin had come between. The eternal problem of atonement was the result. All the other sixty-five books will develop the answer to the eternal question and need here proclaimed. The Book will be written by perhaps more than forty authors over a thousand years or more, but they will never depart from this theme. The story now proceeds rapidly. Sin in chapter 3 has become crime in chapter 4, affecting society and giving us the picture of the making of the criminal class, exemplified by Cain. The treatment of this class by society is expulsion from the group. Chapter 4 ends with civilization progressing by leaps and bounds.

The Generations of Adam, or Man. (5:1—6:8.) These chapters are carefully calculated to bring home the idea that it is not in man to perfect himself. The generations of man are de-generations. A ray of hope comes through Enoch and Noah, but even the most hopeful ones degenerate until the flood is sent to destroy mankind.

The Generations of Noah and His Sons (6:9—11:26) reveal God choosing out a remnant of the race as his fittest redemptive agent. This doctrine is fully exemplified in the familiar story of the flood and the saving of Noah and his family. There is a startling similarity between the promise and opportunity given to Noah in 9:1-7 and that given to Adam and Eve in chapter 1. The natural inability of man is again evidenced when Noah, the one in whom God expected to be comforted, also failed God in the sad ending of chapter 9. In the generations of the sons of Noah which follow, Shem is the favored one and out of his generations come the Semitic strain and the family of Terah, from which God will call Abraham, the father of the faithful.

II. God's Redemptive Purpose Traced from Abraham to Joseph

Genesis 11:27—50:26

The Generations of Terah. (11:27—25:11.) The redemptive purpose of God will now be achieved through the covenant family which God caused to move from Ur of Chaldea to Haran in Mesopotamia. Then came the call of Abram and the promise in chapter 12. Abram was schooled in the process of becoming the father of the faithful. Still unstable, he ran ahead of God as he went into Egypt (12:10-20), and had to go back to Bethel and begin all over (ch. 13). The student should read more about Melchizedek in a Bible dictionary, or in a commentary on chapter 14 and Hebrews 5—7. Covenants and promises continued between God and Abram. In chapter 15 a son was promised and Abram and God "cut a covenant" in blood. But Abram again ran ahead of God. Ishmael was legitimate, to be sure, but he was a "son of the Law." God's chosen one was to be the "son of the Promise." Ishmael was born according to man's plan; Isaac, according to the promise of God. Abram became "Abraham" in chapter 17 with the inauguration of the covenant of circumcision. We hurry past the stories of Abraham and Lot and Sodom and Gomorrah to reach the fruition of the promise of God in the birth of Isaac. (Ch. 21.) The final test of Abraham's faith came in the offering up of Isaac. His peaceful last days are recorded in chapters 22 to 25. The generations of Ishmael (25:12-18) merely tell us of the origin of the desert tribes who will be the proverbial enemies of the Israelites.

The Generations of Isaac (25:19—35:29) bring us the stories of Jacob, the heel-catcher, supplanter, and trickster. Yet God used him to carry out his decree and covenant, working into his plan even the theft of the birthright and blessing from Esau. (Chs. 25—27.) A high point in these narratives is the vision at Bethel where Jacob, in flight, was reassured concerning the Abrahamic covenant. He sojourned in Mesopotamia, married twice, and on his return wrestled with the angel where his name was changed and he became "Israel," the "one who prevailed with God." God has now narrowed his created race down to his peculiar redemptive nation, Israel. The generations of

Esau (ch. 36) are passed over briefly. He will come back into the story frequently, usually as the enemy of his brother Israel.

The Generations of Jacob (37:2—50:26) present in spectacular fashion the hand of God in the history of the Hebrews. If modern readers are slow to admit the sovereign decrees of God, Joseph was not. These stories center around Joseph and his brethren; the sale of Joseph into Egypt; his fortunes and misfortunes there, and his elevation to the office of prime minister. Under his governorship the twelve tribes came into Egypt. Jacob's death and burial and the death of Joseph close the narratives. In 45:5-8, Joseph states that the sovereign decrees of God are brought to pass even through the wrath of man. Genesis leaves the children of Israel in Egypt in the good graces of the government, there to live and multiply for 430 years.

EXODUS

The Emergence of the Redemptive Nation
The Institutions and the Constitution of Israel

Exodus has for its background the bitter political and economic struggle in Egypt. (Ch. 1.) A new Pharaoh had arisen who "knew not Joseph." His policy of oppression naturally resulted in the people's willingness to revolt. God raised up a deliverer, Moses, and through him led out the nation and organized it politically and religiously. Three great institutions form the outline or divisions of this book. The central institution in chapters 1—15 is the Passover; in chapters 16—24, the Law; and in chapters 25—40, the Tabernacle. These institutions are present in most religious groups today. Christian, Jew, and Mohammedan preserve the first one either as the Lord's Supper, the Passover, or the Feast of Lights. All religions recognize the moral law. All have their church edifices whether chapel or cathedral, synagogue or temple, or mosque. Most church architecture also, as was the case of the Tabernacle, is significant. This study of the book of Exodus will be divided into three sections.

I. The Deliverance from Bondage; The Passover

Exodus 1—15

The Birth, Training, and Call of Moses. (Chapters 1—4.) The first chapter presents the sad plight of the children of Israel in Egypt in the fifteenth century B.C. Four hundred years had elapsed since the coming of Jacob and his sons into the land of Goshen. There they multiplied until the inevitable problem of the foreign element about to outnumber the home-born evoked the rigorous policy of extermination.

The student will quickly discern the hand of God in every event connected with the birth and early life of Moses. Reared by Pharaoh's daughter, he would know his way into the official life of Egypt when he returned as deliverer. He was forced by circumstances to flee to the desert. (Ch. 2.) Here he herded sheep for forty years and learned the terrain of the desert of Paran. Later he will use this knowledge to lead his people by these same trails and water courses.

The call of Moses (ch. 3) is preceded by the record of the Pharaoh's death in 2:23. Moses doubtless was convinced that the time to lead out the oppressed people had come. Not only was this a good time, but this desert would be a capital place to organize and mold them into a nation. If God only had the right man! Then it flashed upon him like the flame in the burning bush. Surely this was the very reason for his early training and his present position. Nothing happens by chance. He was God's ordained deliverer. It so overwhelmed him that at first he demurred and was afraid.

The new name for God was given in Exodus 3:14. The occasion was the assurance to Moses of God's eternal presence and power. "When I come unto the children of Israel, and shall say unto them, The God of your fathers hath sent me unto you; and they shall say to me, What is his name? what shall I say unto them?" A name is what you are. Jacob and Esau were named because of their outstanding characteristics. Abraham's name was significant. Moses was asking, "When I tell the people about the God of our fathers, those poor souls in bondage and oppression are going to ask, 'What is that God of our fathers to *us now* in our plight?' " God recognized the

importance of the question. His answer proclaimed, "I AM THAT I AM
. . . this is my name for ever." (3:14-15.) No one seems to know
exactly the original Name. It is evidently made from the verb "to
be" in the Hebrew. It is written usually in four Hebrew letters which
translated read JHVH. Original Hebrew had no vowels. The ancients
so revered the Ineffable Name that they declared that it should never
be pronounced. When they encountered the four letters they rev-
erently said "Adonai" (My Lord). Later the vowels from Adonai
were incorporated into JHVH, giving us our word "Jehovah" (LORD).
We do not know how it should be pronounced. Various translations
are "I Am Because I Am," or "I Am Who Am," or "I Will Be That
I Will Be." It means that God is eternally the same to his people;
that he will be to them whatever it is necessary that he shall be; and
that what he is he will eternally be and do. Confirmatory signs
(ch. 4) convinced Moses, and he and Aaron determined to go to the
Pharaoh with the demand for the release of the captives.

Moses and Aaron Before the Pharaoh. (Chapters 5—11.) The demands of Moses, accompanied by miraculous signs, only caused the
Pharaoh to become more stubborn. There followed the plagues of
Egypt. The first four merely brought discomfort. The next four
brought destruction to the cattle and the fields of Egypt. The ninth
was a plague of terror, a fitting forerunner to the plague of death.
Several times the Pharaoh relented and then hardened his heart again
when relief came. Finally after he had hardened his own heart so
often, we are told that "the LORD hardened Pharaoh's heart." It was
in preparation for the terrible judgment upon Egypt and Israel's deliverance therefrom that God's people were given the Passover.

The Passover. (12:1-28.) This great prototype of deliverance from
judgment through the blood of a slain Lamb is observed by Jew and
Christian to this day. Jesus celebrated the Passover with his disciples
on the night before his death, and at the close of it, declared himself
to be the fulfillment of it as he instituted the Lord's Supper. Following the "As-So" method of teaching of the scribes of Israel, we see
the antetype of the Christ signified in the Passover:

AS	SO
1. Israel is to choose a lamb without blemish	"Behold the Lamb of God!" (John 1:36)
2. It is to be slain as a sacrifice	Jesus is sacrificed for our sins.
3. The blood is to be displayed as protection from judgment	We are saved by the blood of the Christ.
4. It is to be completely consumed	Jesus gives himself to the uttermost.
5. Not a bone of the lamb is to be broken	"When they came to Jesus . . . they brake not his legs . . . that the scripture might be fulfilled, A bone of him shall not be broken." (John 19:33-36)
6. They must remain indoors till morning	We take shelter behind the blood of the crucified One.
7. The Angel of Death passed over those who displayed the blood	"There is therefore now no condemnation to them that are in Christ Jesus." (Romans 8:1)

The Last Plague and the Exodus. (12:29—15:27.) The death of the first-born in every house and among all living creatures brought the king of Egypt to his knees. Moses led out a great host, reported at six hundred thousand men on foot, besides women and children. The first-born of Israel were consecrated to God as a memorial of their deliverance. The destruction of Pharaoh's army and the song of Moses and Miriam close this section; but not without an ominous murmuring on the part of the disorganized people.

II. THE HEBREW STATE; THE LAW

Exodus 16—24

The Organization of a Representative Democracy. (Chapters 16—18.) Two momentous events are described in this section: the organization of the Hebrew state, and the giving of the Ten Commandments. Events in chapters 16 and 17 indicated the necessity for organization. The murmuring of the people and the encountering of enemies in war emphasized the fact that a one-man government would be an insurmountable task. Credit for the organization of the Hebrew state goes to Jethro, Moses' father-in-law, a priest of Midian. Impressed by the impossibility of Moses' carrying the entire burden, Jethro advised the choosing of representative rulers from the people—rulers over tens, fifties, hundreds, and thousands with a gradation of courts and the right of appeal. Thus through a representative democracy, government would be of the people and by the people. This state government parallels our republican form of government today.

The Law of Mount Sinai. (Chapters 19—23.) With infinite precaution God charged Moses to prepare the people to receive "the Law." We not only should learn the words of the Ten Commandments, but should also recognize their significance as a rule of faith and practice given to God's chosen people. Jesus himself declared, "Till heaven and earth pass away, one jot or one tittle shall in no wise pass away from the law." (Matt. 5:18.) He said to the lawyer who gave the summation of the Law, "This do, and thou shalt live." (Luke 10:25-28.) The Ten Commandments are generally divided into two tables: that which is our duty (due-to) to God in commandments 1-4, and our duty (due-to) to our fellow man in commandments 5-10. Exodus 20:1-17 gives the Ten Commandments in their original form. Chapters 21—23 are various statutes based upon the original ten. They probably were added as national and social life developed. This whole section (chs. 20—24) is sometimes called C, the Covenant. After Moses had ratified and confirmed this covenant in blood (24:1-8) he departed again into the mount to receive the Law on tables of stone. While he was on the mount this second time God gave him the plan for the Tabernacle.

III. GOD'S DWELLING PLACE: THE TABERNACLE

Exodus 25—40

The Pattern for the Sanctuary. (Chapters 25—27.) The student should consult the Westminster Bible dictionary for a picture of the individual furniture and the arrangement of the Tabernacle. It was erected from the freewill offerings of the people—a sanctuary or place for God to dwell. Some believe that a rather simple tent of meeting was erected and transported through the wilderness, while the more elaborate Tabernacle, perfect in detail and rich in furnishings, was completed after Israel had become a settled nation.

The chief point of interest is the significance of the arrangement. God was within the veil, shut off from the worshipers. Just outside the heavy veil was the altar of incense (prayers). The showbread on the table on one side and the seven-branched candlestick on the other signified the Bread of Life and the Light of the World. Outside the tent in the open court stood the laver, and near the gate of the court was a large altar for burnt offerings.

Imagine the worshiper approaching God from without. It is the picturization of access to God. The anointed priest met the worshiper at the entrance and offered his sacrifice for him. The priest then washed himself at the laver, changed his clothes, and went into the Holy Place—the place of the Bread of Life and the Light of the World, and the place of prayer. Only once a year on the Day of Atonement, and then "not without blood," did the high priest enter the Holy of Holies within the veil, there to make atonement for the nation. Access to God, then, is by way of sacrifice, cleanliness, and prayer, through the mediation of the God-appointed priest.

The Priests and Their Offerings. (Chapters 28—31.) Aaron and his sons were designated as the priests chosen to minister in the Tabernacle. Their robes of office were elaborate and significant, the high priest wearing the names of the twelve tribes on his shoulders and over his heart. The consecration of the priests in chapter 29 rivaled the elaborate ceremonies in some liturgical churches today. Offerings were provided for the service of the sanctuary. Having completed the plans for the Tabernacle, God gave to Moses that for which he had ascended the mount the second time, "the two tables of the testimony, tables of stone, written with the finger of God."

Sin in the Camp: The Golden Calf. (Chapters 32—34.) The type of idolatry practiced in the worship of the little golden bull that Aaron fashioned is traceable to the heathen rites that the Israelites had witnessed in Egypt. Evidently there were foreigners from Egypt who had attached themselves to the Israelites when they departed. Aaron was not entirely insensible to his own God. Even though he fashioned the idol and sanctioned the immoral idolatry, he still proclaimed it as a worship of or a "feast to the LORD." (32:5.)

Here occurs one of the examples of "anthropomorphism" in the Pentateuch—that is, speaking of God in terms applicable to man. God is made to have thoughts, anger, passions, and impatience as any human being would. In 32:7-14 he is represented as having lost all patience with his people and being ready to destroy them. He will make of Moses another nation. Moses must pacify the angry God. This he did by convincing God that it was incompatible with his character to do such a thing, referring to them as "thy people, that thou hast brought forth out of the land of Egypt with great power and with a mighty hand." Moreover the Egyptians would declare that Jehovah had brought forth his people to slay them and not to deliver them. Finally and climactically, he reminded Jehovah that he had made a covenant with Abraham, Isaac, and Jacob. Surely the God of the Hebrews is a covenant-keeping God. In the face of this solemn and convincing argument, Jehovah relented (the Scripture says, "repented of the evil which he said he would do") and turned again to his people.

Following the punishment of the people for their idolatry, the prayers and persuasions of Moses again prevailed upon God and assured his leadership. The story in 33:17—34:9 is another anthropomorphic passage. Moses saw God! Encouraged by God's declaration of his favor toward him, Moses presumed to ask God that he might see his face. Hid in a cleft of the rock he was allowed to see God's "back" as he covered the cleft in the rock with his "hand" and passed by. What Moses "saw" was what transpired or followed when God passed by. He saw "a God merciful and gracious, slow to anger, and abundant in lovingkindness and truth; keeping lovingkindness for thousands, forgiving iniquity and transgression and sin; and that will by no means clear the guilty." (34:6-7.) God then repeated the covenant and gave Moses the second edition of the tables of stone called now the Ten Commandments.

The Construction and Erection of the Tabernacle. (Chapters 35—

40.) The Tent and its furniture were now manufactured according to the pattern. Moses inspected the finished work, and the Tabernacle in the wilderness was raised on the first day of the first month of the second year. The pillar of cloud and fire—emblem of the presence of Jehovah—hovered over his sanctuary.

LEVITICUS

Access to God

Exodus closed with the covenant people shut out from the presence of God by the very arrangement of the Tabernacle. Leviticus will show how access to God may be effected, and how this "separation to God" may be maintained. Separation means holiness. Many scholars believe that Leviticus is composed of a number of priestly codes or documents compiled by an editor. The content of the book provides two principal studies.

I. ACCESS TO GOD ATTAINED THROUGH ATONEMENT

Leviticus 1—17

The Sacrifices of Israel. (Chapters 1—7.) The people achieve access to God through sacrifice which makes "at-one-ment." There are five principal sacrifices. The whole burnt offering (ch. 1); the meal offering (the King James Version says "meat" offering) (ch. 2); and the peace offering (ch. 3), all carry the idea of communion with God and are intended to express thanksgiving or consecration. The sin offering (4:1—5:13) and the trespass offering (5:14—6:7) are for sins and trespasses done unwittingly; that is, without premeditation. For premeditated sins no offering was provided. (See Hebrews 10: 26-31.) These last two sacrifices carried the idea of expiation for guilt because of sins and for trespasses or damage done to God's holy things or to one's fellow. In case of damage, the offender must not only offer sacrifice, but must restore the actual value of the thing destroyed plus one-fifth of the value thereof. Every sacrifice must be unblemished and of the very best, for they typify the perfect sacrifice of him who makes atonement and expiation for our sins. The directions to the priests for the proper performance of these rites and sacrifices comprise a complete manual of forms. (6:8— 7:38.) The wave offering and the heave offering were the portions of the sacrifices reserved for the priests, who lived from the offerings of the people.

The Consecration of the Priests. (Chapters 8—10.) Aaron and his sons were publicly inducted into office in a ritual that was to be a precedent for later generations of priests. It was elaborate and was comparable to the ordination of ministers. Following their consecration they were required to offer each of the principal sacrifices in turn. At the conclusion God evidenced his pleasure and presence by miraculously lighting the fire on the altar. The priests tended this sacred fire continuously thenceforth.

The interruption in chapter 10 describes the sin and punishment of Nadab and Abihu, sons of Aaron who were slain by lightning for offering strange fire. With the sacred fire provided for them, they failed to make a distinction between the sacred and the profane! This is one of the two narrative portions which occur in this book of priestly codes and ceremonies. (See also ch. 24.) Both are punishments for breaches of the codes. The story is emphatic in its teaching and carries with it the first "prohibition" statute in the Old Testament. From henceforth the priests were not permitted to drink wine during the time of the discharge of their priestly functions. Evidently the two young priests were drunk when they so transgressed.

The Laws of Purity. (Chapters 11—17.) Access to God up to this point has been through sacrifice and the mediation of the consecrated priesthood. It was further necessary that the worshiper keep himself pure. Chapter 11 contains the Pure Food Laws of Israel. The fact that an orthodox Hebrew will not eat pork is only one detail among the prohibitions of unclean foods. Any four-footed beast, to be edible, must have a split-hoof and chew the cud. Acceptable fish must have both fins and scales, thus restricting the diet to game fish which live in running waters and ordinarily eat living food. Birds of prey were all excluded, and creeping things, to be eaten, must belong to the family of grasshoppers and locusts. Sensibly considered, these were sanitary laws and precautions, enforced by a religious taboo.

Control of Disease. (Chapters 12—15.) The sanitary precautions outlined in these chapters were quite advanced. The religious or ceremonial uncleanness that kept mothers of newborn babes secluded from society for a time protected both mother and child. Mary, mother of Jesus, offered the sacrifice prescribed here at the birth of her Son. (Luke 2:22-24.) Leprosy was considered incurable. It was rigidly quarantined, and in the case of a recovery, which in the very nature of the disease must be miraculous, elaborate thanksgiving sacrifice was provided. (Matt. 8:2-4.) Laws for the cleansing of infected houses and for ceremonial uncleanness not only protected the people and controlled the spread of disease, but constantly reminded them of the sacredness and holiness of their God.

The Great Day of Atonement. (Chapter 16.) The Passover and the great Day of Atonement, "Yom Kippur," are the two great days of the Jewish sacred year. The Day of Atonement is celebrated annually on the tenth day of the seventh month, about September, as a day of humiliation and repentance for all sins confessed and unconfessed. Why did Israel need such a day? They had already offered a sacrifice for every type of sin which they confessed to the priest. But the consciousness of sin is never equal to the sin itself. Hence some sins would be left unconfessed. The people, called to their knees once a year in humble contrition, could confess directly to God what they would be reluctant to confess to a human mediator. Here is a beginning of the idea of the universal priesthood of believers. It was also a great social leveler. Kings and peasants, priests and people, were all on the same plane—sinners needing atonement.

The ceremonial was spectacular and significant. The two-goat ceremony is another Old Testament prototype of the work of the Redeemer. He was made "the Goat, the Scapegoat" for us. The first goat on which the lot for death fell was sacrificed for the sins of the people. The priest then confessed the sins over the head of the goat for Azazel, or escape. Immediately it was led away and released in the wilderness so far distant that it could not return to the camp.

There were evidenced here the two features in the atoning work of the Saviour. He died for our sins and "He hath borne our griefs, and carried our sorrows . . . and the LORD hath laid on him the iniquity of us all." (Isa. 53:4-6.) "As far as the east is from the west, so far hath he removed our transgressions from us." (Ps. 103:12.)

Blood was used to make atonement. Hence it was sacred. (Lev. 17: 1-14.) The laws placing the slaughtering of animals and the prohibition of the eating of blood on a religious basis were both practical and sacred: practical for health reasons, and sacred for the sake of enforcement. Orthodox Jews still regard this prohibition in their habits of daily living.

II. ACCESS TO GOD MAINTAINED THROUGH HOLINESS

Leviticus 18—27

The Holiness Code. (Chapters 18—20.) Holiness means separation. The idea here was not only separation to God, but separation from evil. The key to the section, often repeated, is found in the expression, "Ye shall be holy; for I the LORD your God am holy." God had brought them out of Egypt. They were en route to lands equally godless. If they were to maintain their at-one-ment with God, they must keep themselves separate from any such "doings" as were practiced by these godless nations. (18:3-5.) This section is sometimes called H, or the Holiness Code. Ezekiel used it in picturing his New Jerusalem. The first group of these laws was an attempt to set the bounds of consanguinity in marriage. Two things have always manifested themselves in the relation of man to woman: either the high and holy relation exhibited in pure marriage, like unto the relation between Jesus and his church; or, on the other hand, the greatest manifestation of wickedness. God's people must hold this relationship as different, holy, and sacred. Crimes of violence, unchastity, idol worship, and human sacrifice were specifically forbidden in chapters 19—20. Especially noteworthy is the advance made in 19:18, "Thou shalt not take vengeance, nor bear any grudge against the children of thy people; but thou shalt love thy neighbor as thyself."

The Exemplary Life of the Priests. (21:1—22:16.) The priests were holy. They must therefore live differently, and on a basis separate from the average man. They stood as God's representatives: "the consecration of the anointing oil of his God is upon him." (21:12, margin.) Prohibitions and requirements were laid down regarding their life, behavior, and marriage. Even physical defects barred one from the priesthood. There was no intimation of unworthiness in bodily defects, but God's ministry must be embellished with our best and holiest. Inasmuch as the priests were also fallible, provisions were made for their own sacrifices and atonements. Like the character of the priests was the character of the offerings over which they officiated. Every offering must be from the best of the flock or herd, "perfect . . . there shall be no blemish therein." (22:17-33.) The sacrifices were typical of the one great Sacrifice that was one day to be offered for our sins. He was holy, harmless, and undefiled. God's messenger, Malachi, properly called down a righteous judgment upon "the deceiver, who hath in his flock a male, and voweth, and sacrificeth unto the Lord a blemished thing; for I am a great King, saith the LORD of hosts." (Mal.1:14.)

The Stated Meetings of the Assembly. (Chapter 23.) Besides the Sabbath, five other great feasts, or regular assemblies, marked Israel's religious life: the Passover, Pentecost (or feast of weeks), the Trumpets, the Day of Atonement, and the Feast of the Tabernacles which was inaugurated after the wilderness wanderings. Israel looked forward to these great gatherings and valued them. We should never make our coming before the Lord so common that our assemblies lose their value.

The Law of Consecration, and the Punishment for Blasphemy. (Chapter 24.) In the midst of the interesting specifications for the ministry of the table of the showbread and the oil of the sanctuary there occurs the second of the two narrative portions in Leviticus. It has to do with the punishment for blasphemy and the vain use of the Ineffable Name. (Exod. 3:14 and 20:7.) So unusual was this breach of the Law that there was no precedent for punishment. The sentence of death imposed on the blasphemer by order of God should give us sober pause. The very Name must also be kept holy. The writer seems to seek some extenuation of the crime in the fact that the offender had an Egyptian father. The conclusion to this passage brings us the famous *"lex talionis,"* an eye for an eye and a tooth for a tooth.

The Law of Rest. (Chapter 25.) Moses' people had been serfs in Egypt. This is evidently why he gave such emphasis to the Sabbatical laws. The Sabbatic Year first observed in Exodus 21 as applicable to slaves was now made to apply to the very fields and vineyards. Modern agriculture has learned the value of using land wisely and rotating crops. Every seventh Sabbatical year, the forty-ninth, was preparatory to the great double Sabbath for land and people—a fiftieth Year of Jubilee, in which land reverted to the original owner and all debts were canceled. Justice in dealing was insured by making all sales in reality leases which must run only to the next Year of Jubilee. Anticipating the skepticism of some and the avarice of others, God emphatically promised them security if they would faithfully keep these periods of rest. (25:20-22.) The right of redemption of property by kinsmen and the forbidding of interest charges reappear in Ruth, chapters 3—4, and in Nehemiah, chapter 5. (Dummelow, pp. 99-100.)

The Law of Obedience and Disobedience. (Chapter 26.) Man is always the chooser. God set before his people the blessing and the curse; the reward for obedience and the penalty for disobedience. Standing ready to begin their journey to Canaan, they were made to face the sobering alternatives. Chapter 26:3-13 recounts the generous blessings of obedience: verses 14-45 hold before them the fearful consequences of disobedience, with the indication in verses 44-45 that God knew already that his people would disobey, and that he had already planned for their recovery after their punishment. This chapter brings to an end "the statutes and ordinances and laws, which the LORD made between him and the children of Israel in mount Sinai by Moses."

The Law of Vows and Consecrated Things. (Chapter 27.) This section seems to have been added after the conclusion of the book noted above. It teaches that those things which had been "separated to God" might not be carelessly taken back. They were holy. Gradations of penalties were made according to the age and sex of the offenders. Money substitutes were provided for consecrated fields, introducing a sort of original God's-acre plan. The tithe was insisted upon and any change of the thing promised or consecrated for one of lesser value cost the worshiper both the one promised and the one substituted.

The nation has been constituted and has been shown the way of access to God and the maintenance thereof. They stand now ready to begin the promised journey to the Promised Land.

NUMBERS

The Discipline of the Redemptive Nation

Numbers is so called because of the census or numbering of the people which occurs twice in the book. After two years of organization and emphasis on the Law and the sacrifices, God's covenant people should have been ready to move into their inheritance. Experiences proved, however, that they were not yet ready. The next forty years was a training or disciplinary period on the basis of the laws given at Sinai. Another generation had to pass away before Joshua led them across Jordan. The story of Numbers is the journey from Sinai to the Promised Land, which is presented in the two following studies.

I. THE JOURNEY TOWARD THE GOAL

Numbers 1:1—20:13

Directions for the Journey. (1:1—10:10.) The census in chapter 1 showed 603,550 fighting men, exclusive of the small tribe of Levi, reserved for the priesthood. A permanent arrangement for the camp was set up which insured the location of any tribe at all times. The special religious significance of the arrangement lay in the fact that Jehovah was in the midst; that is, the Tabernacle and surrounding tents of the Levites occupied a central position. The Levites were at this time officially designated as the priestly tribe, replacing the first-born of every tribe who were consecrated to God's service by the law of Exodus 13. God conferred this honor on the tribe of Moses and Aaron. It also had the virtue of expediency, inasmuch as this small tribe could be readily available. The males were numbered from a month old and upward. Three Levitical clans divided the work of the Tabernacle (chs. 3—4) and exercised an active priesthood from the ages of thirty to fifty.

The laws of Numbers (ch. 5) excluded from the camp everything that was unclean, including the lepers and those afflicted with infectious diseases. Rules for the expiation of guilt were introduced. The strange law of jealousy bore a resemblance to later ordeals for the establishment of guilt or innocence. A double standard still prevailed, and no such law was commanded for the men. Woman will, however, be elevated more and more as the working out of the Mosaic law proceeds.

The Nazirite vow (ch. 6) indicated separation to service. The verb *nazar* means to separate. Hence the Nazirite is one separated or devoted to God. During the days of his separation he scrupulously observed three prohibitions: he must not touch wine or strong drink; he must not shave his head; and he must not render himself ceremonially unclean by touching a dead body. Originally it signified a lifelong obligation, but was later modified to cover set periods of consecration. It was also expanded to include women; the prophetess Anna was probably a Nazirite. (Luke 2:36-37.) Samson and Samuel were outstanding examples of men set apart by this vow taken by their mothers.

One of the best-known and best-loved benedictions is the "priestly benediction" of 6:24-26, to be used officially in putting the name of the Lord upon the Children of Israel. It is a fine parallel to the "apostolic benediction" given by Paul in II Corinthians 13:14 and generally used in Christian churches. The priestly benediction is heard regularly in Jewish synagogues and temples today.

Each tribe had a census enumerator designated as prince. (1:4-16.) Now they came to Moses (ch. 7) with a surprise gift: six covered wagons drawn by six yoke of oxen, bearing all manner of utensils and provisions for the service of the Tabernacle. Moses dedicated them and divided the wagons and oxen among two clans of the

Levites who had the duty of hauling the Tabernacle and its boards
and walls. The Kohathites received no wagon since they bore the
sacred furniture upon their shoulders. The lighting of the seven-
branched candlestick by Aaron and the official consecration of the
Levites (ch. 8) completely furnished and prepared the Tabernacle
for service. The Passover was celebrated preparatory to the departure (ch. 9) and provision was made for a "Little Passover," or de-
layed celebration for those who were ceremonially prohibited from
the general celebration. Immediate preparation consisted in the
presence of the pillar of cloud and fire, the guide for the journey.

From Sinai to Kadesh-Barnea: Three Failures. (10:11—14:45.)
With dramatic suddenness, early in the second year, the cloud rose
from the Tabernacle. The trumpets called the assembly. According
to plan the tribes arranged themselves for the march. Moses insisted
on the company of Hobab, his brother-in-law,* who finally agreed to
guide them. (Judges 4:11.) The two sayings of Moses found in 10:
35-36 are also incorporated into Psalm 68.

Three failures marred the pilgrimage, and each brought its penalty.
The first was the murmuring of the people for meat and the consequences. (Ch. 11.) Moses had remonstrated repeatedly because of
this and God sent a fire as a warning. But they rebelled again, longing for the fleshpots of Egypt. Moses for the first time lost patience.
In this instance of anthropomorphism Moses waxed angry and
practically rebuked God. (11:10-15.) God was most patient with
him and in answer to the complaint that he was not able to bear
the burden of the people alone, appointed the seventy elders. These
seventy elders chosen from among the people were ordained, or in-
spirited, to be the rulers of the congregation. God then sent quail to
the hungry murmurers, for the space of thirty days. They slaughtered and ate the quail until great numbers were sickened and died.

The second failure (12:1-15) involved the leaders. Jealousy, incited by resentment against Moses' second wife, led Miriam and
Aaron to question his leadership. God's rebuke was stern. Miriam
was smitten with leprosy and healed only after the prayers of both
brothers and the punishment of quarantine and humiliation.

---

* A.S.V. margin, as well as R.S.V. and K.J.V., read father-in-law.

The third failure brought disaster. (12:16—14:45.) Twelve spies were sent across the southern boundary of the Promised Land. Only Joshua and Caleb had faith to believe that Israel could conquer the fierce native tribes. Led by the other ten spies the incensed multitude mutinied and attempted to stone Joshua and Caleb, choose a new leader, and return to Egypt. Now the Lord is represented as losing patience. He threatened to destroy Israel and make of Moses a new nation. The magnificent prayer of Moses allayed the anger of God and brought forgiveness. As punishment the forty years of wilderness wandering was decreed. Saddened and disheartened, the people made a vain attempt to enter Canaan and were beaten back into the wilderness to wander until another generation should perish.

The Period of Wandering. (15:1—20:13.) The next thirty-eight years were fraught with calamity. The laws were carefully repeated for the sake of the rising generation. But sin was imbedded in the people. In the face of the repetition of laws came a flagrant case of Sabbath breaking, and capital punishment—merely for picking up a bundle of sticks on the Sabbath. The penalty had to be severe to emphasize the necessity of absolute obedience. Here originated the fringes and "cord of blue" on the borders of the garments of the Israelites, to remind them that the Law must be kept. The phylacteries of New Testament times and the prayer shawls in synagogues today are relics of this custom.

The rebellion of Korah and the story of Aaron's rod (chs. 16—18) confirmed the priestly superiority of Aaron. God intervened by an earthquake and engulfed the pretenders to the priesthood. Korah's company of 250 princes who offered incense were devoured by fire. Their brazen censers, recovered from the ashes, were hammered into a covering for the altar in the Tabernacle court—a silent warning against revolution or attempted usurpation of the Levitical office. Still the people rebelled. God sent a killing plague. Aaron, with his censer filled with fire from the sacred altar, stood between his people and destruction as he made atonement for them—a dramatic prototype of our great High Priest who made eternal atonement for us and stands between us and judgment. Approximately 15,000 died in the plague. The rebellious generation was rapidly passing away.

The period of wandering came to an end with the people back at the starting point of Kadesh-Barnea. There Miriam died. Even Moses defaulted and was placed under penalty of exclusion. His sin (20:2-13) was not merely an act of disobedience. It was the failure to give God the glory for bringing the water from the smitten rock (Num. 27:14 and Deut. 32:51), and, worse, the lack of faith in God's power or willingness to bear longer with these "rebels" (Num. 20: 10, 12).

II. THE GOAL IN SIGHT; PREPARATION FOR THE CONQUEST OF CANAAN

Numbers 20:14—36:13

From Kadesh-Barnea to the Plains of Moab. (Chapters 20—21.) Edom (Esau) now repaid the trickery of his brother Israel (Jacob) by refusing him passage into Moab. The tribes were forced to go around the Mount Seir range. Aaron died and Eleazar was appointed his successor. Moses led around the mountains, met and conquered Arad, and again the people murmured because of the hardships along the way. The sending of the fiery serpents and the lifting up of the brazen serpent as the cure for the stricken people furnishes another great Old Testament prototype of Messianic deliverance. After reading this story (21:4-9), the student should read Jesus' interview with Nicodemus (John 3:14-16), in which Jesus again used the "As-So" method of his predecessors:

AS	*SO*
Israel was bitten by the serpent . . .	The world is bitten by sin.
The bite of the serpent was death . . .	The wages of sin is death.
Moses "lifts up" a brazen serpent, made in the image of the poisonous ones, but harmless . . .	Even so must the Son of Man (born in the image of sinful man, but sinless) be lifted up.
Those who looked to it lived . . .	"That whosoever believeth on him should not perish, but have eternal life." (Those who look to him, live.)

The Plains of Moab: The Wanderings Over. (22:1—36:13.) Balak, king of Moab, attempted to hire Balaam, the prophet, to curse Israel. (22:2—ch. 25.) Balaam evidently came from the same religious background as did Israel. He is the first of the Old Testament soothsayers and stands as the type of prophet who toys with his conscience and sells out for the wages of men. His attempts to curse Israel were changed to blessings in his mouth, closing finally with a Messianic promise. (24:17.)

The second census (ch. 26) showed the remarkable fact that despite the rigors of the wilderness wanderings the number of men was only 1,820 less than in chapter 1. This census was made for the purpose of alloting fairly the land across the Jordan. In this connection the law of female inheritance (27:1-11) was another step in the recognition of the status of woman. Warned of his approaching death and with Joshua appointed as his successor (27:12-23), Moses repeated the laws of the various offerings to be observed in the new era of national life (chs. 28—30).

The settlement of the East Jordan tribes followed the conquest of the Midianites and the division of the spoils. (Chs. 31—32.) The tribes of Reuben, Gad, and one-half Manasseh asked the privilege of settling east of Jordan due to the fact that the East-Jordan plateau offered splendid grazing land for their cattle. Moses at first indignantly refused, accusing them of unwillingness to bear the brunt of the invasion with their brethren. Upon their promise to form the vanguard for the invasion, Moses declared that these two and a half tribes should occupy the East Jordan plateau. Joshua witnessed the pact. (Ch. 32.) The West Jordan tribes never felt kindly toward these who entered not into the Promised Land, and interesting repercussions followed. (Joshua 22.)

Maps of the wilderness wanderings are usually made from Numbers 33:1-49 where the journey is specifically detailed. The failure of the tribes to carry out the harsh instructions regarding the conquest of Canaan (33:50-56) was declared by the writer of Judges to be the key to Israel's misfortunes during that period (Judges 2:1-5). An advance over the law of retaliation was instituted in the Cities of Refuge, three on each side of the Jordan, where the manslayer might flee for refuge and a trial. Here was the beginning of the definition of murder and manslaughter. (35:16-34.)

The law of female inheritance (ch. 26) brought difficulties when an heiress married, for her property immediately belonged to her husband. Where the husband belonged to another tribe it necessarily meant that tribal lines were in constant danger of being moved. To simplify this difficulty, the command was issued that heiresses must marry into families of their own tribe. Numbers 36:13 states that Moses' work of leadership and law-giving ended in the plain of Moab with the giving of these commandments and ordinances.

DEUTERONOMY

The Repetition of the Law

The traditional belief holds that we have here, after the introduction, the last three addresses of Moses, delivered east of Jordan preparatory to entering the Promised Land. The addresses reviewed the Journey, the Law, and the Covenant, respectively. They are intended to go over Israel's past experiences with a view to gathering out of them strength for the task ahead of the nation. The date would then be about 1450 B.C. Obviously it was put into the present form by some later writer, who concluded by telling of the death of Moses and writing a remarkable tribute to him.

The theory held by a large number of scholars regarding the age and authorship of Deuteronomy connects its origin with the story in II Kings 22—23 and II Chronicles 34—35. These chapters record that during the repairing of the Temple under the boy king Josiah, Hilkiah the famous high priest "found" this book of the Law of Jehovah given by Moses. Hilkiah informed Shaphan the Scribe of his discovery. They took their discovery to Huldah the Prophetess to have her attest its genuineness. Huldah declared it to be the very Word of God, and the three then took it to the young king. He, conscience-stricken, called a solemn assembly and had the Book with its solemn promises and warnings publicly read and adopted by the people. There followed a great revival. This took place about 621 B.C.*

Some scholars declare that Deuteronomy is merely the recoding by eighth- or seventh-century religious leaders of the three former books of Moses. Taking advantage of the literary awakening and the general revival under Josiah, they saw here a fine opportunity to revive the Law of Moses which had been so woefully neglected under the reigns of Manasseh and Amon. So their "finding" the Book was in reality their own compiling of it—or making it public after a period of safekeeping during the reigns of the evil kings. They assigned it to Moses because they believed it to be a restatement of Mosaic Law in terms that spoke to their day, and because that would be the only means of giving it authority in lawless Israel.

I. THE FIRST ADDRESS: THE REVIEW OF THE JOURNEY

Deuteronomy 1:6—4:49

The first address summarizes the events from the departure from Sinai to the arrival in Moab. Emphasis is put upon the failures of the people and their rebellious spirit. (Ch. 1.) It is told in the first person, and Moses confesses his own sin and failure. (3:23-29.) The address concludes with a plea (ch. 4) to observe God's Law: first, because it is righteous; second, because it was given immediately and personally by him; third, because Jehovah is a jealous God; fourth, because he is a merciful God; and last, because he is a loving God.

II. THE SECOND ADDRESS: THE REVIEW OF THE LAW

Deuteronomy 5:1—26:19

The Rehearsal of the Ten Commandments. (5:1-21.) This section (chs. 5—26) forms the bulk of the book and gives it the title "Deuteronomy," or "The Repetition of the Law." The Ten Commandments given here follow the order and wording of Exodus 20 with certain

---

* For different views on the age and authorship of Deuteronomy, consult Raven: *Introduction to the Old Testament*, and Driver: *An Introduction to the Literature of the Old Testament*. The latter was reissued in a paperback edition in 1956.

exceptions in the fourth and tenth. The reason for observing the Sabbath here is different. (5:12-15.) In Exodus the Sabbath was hallowed
because of the example and command of God. In Deuteronomy it is
in order that the servant classes may have rest, calling attention to
their own servitude in Egypt. The change in the tenth command-
ment gives prominence to the place of the wife. These variations
have led some to believe that they are from a later date when Israel
was living in settled homes with servant classes.

Exposition of the First Table of the Law. (6:4—16:17.) This review enlarges upon the first four commandments—man's spiritual
relationship to God—opening with the famous "Shema" ("Hear, O
Israel"), 6:4, which was taught to the babes as soon as they learned
to lisp their prayers. Here was the beginning of religious education
in the home. (Ch. 6.) Orthodox Jews today follow this precept concerning the sign upon the hand, the frontlets between the eyes in the
family devotions, and the little "mezuzah," fastened to the doorpost,
containing this and other portions of Scripture and the Holy Name.
The rehearsal of Jehovah's gracious dealings and the story of the two
tables of the Law occupy chapters 7:1—10:11. The definite location
of, and directions concerning, Mounts Ebal and Gerizim, which
Moses never saw, and the directions for a central sanctuary (12:5),
indicate a West Jordan acquaintance on the part of the writer. Drastic punishment was to be meted out to the false prophet. (Ch. 13 and
18:20-22.) False prophets were prominent in the seventh century
B. C. at the time of Jeremiah and Hilkiah. Repetition of the laws of
Leviticus touching Sabbatic years, tithes, and feasts conclude this
exposition. (15:1—16:17.)

Exposition of the Second Table of the Law. (16:18—26:16.) The
laws given for the official administration of state government (16:
18—21:23) were evidently given for the people's settled national life.
Of outstanding interest is the law for the king. (17:14-20.) Israel did
not have a king until 350 years after Moses. The three types of kings
here warned against bear remarkable resemblance to Saul, David,
and Solomon, whose reigns were failures in these respects. Hezekiah,
in the eighth century, would fit the picture of the democratic law-
abiding monarch described in verses 18-20. This section stands as a

solemn basis for godly civil government today. New rules for exemption in military service appear in chapter 20, including the newly married, new home builders, farmers, and husbandmen. Another advance in the status of women which formed the basis for the argument between Jesus and his critics (Matt. 19:7-9) was the law of the "bill of divorcement" (24: 1-4). This was especially for the protection of the woman in the midst of prevailing Asiatic marriage customs. The second address is rounded out with a carefully worded conclusion. (26:16-19.)

III. THE THIRD ADDRESS: THE REVIEW OF THE COVENANT

Deuteronomy 27—33

The Covenant to Be Renewed at Mounts Ebal and Gerizim. (27: 1—31:13.) This address opens with the command to renew the covenant at Mounts Ebal and Gerizim. These mountains rose on either side of the little city of Shechem, making a natural amphitheater. Here Israel would later meet for the coronation of their kings. (Judges 9:1; I Kings 12:1.) Here the only instance of fable in the Bible was told by the outraged Jotham, son of Gideon. (Judges 9: 7-21.)

The Levites stood in the center of the bowl to pronounce the blessings and the curses, and six tribes stood on either slope to shout "Amen." Each of these curses was aimed at some sin practiced by the nations that Israel was to dislodge. The writer shows intimate knowledge of the nations who inhabited the land west of the Jordan.

The blessings of obedience and the fearful consequences of disobedience (Lev. 26) are extended here in detail (Deut. 28). Anticipating rebellion, the solemn Moab covenant (29:1—31:13) emphasized the fact that it was not merely for those present, but for generations unborn.

The Completion of Moses' Task. (31:14—33:29.) Moses' final charge at the ripe age of one hundred and twenty commended the people to God and charged that this Law be read publicly every seventh year at the Feast of Tabernacles. (See Neh. 8:2.) His last act was to lay it up beside the Ark of the Covenant as a witness against the people.

Warned of his approaching death, and with Joshua already designated to succeed him, Moses was commanded to write a song to remind the people of their heritage and warn them against apostasy. (31:19-22.) The Song or Psalm of Moses (32:1-43), is divided into four movements, or poetical recollections:

1. The Creation and Exaltation of Israel. 32:1-14.
2. Their Ingratitude and Apostasy. 32:15-18.
3. Israel Forsaken and Scattered. 32:19-25.
4. Israel Redeemed and Saved. 32:26-43.

Moses was summoned on that same day to ascend Mount Nebo and view the Promised Land which he might not enter. Chapter 33 contains Moses' blessing, in which, like the patriarchs of old, he prophetically blessed each tribe by name, and with a final word breathed a blessing on his entire beloved people.

IV. THE DEATH OF MOSES: AN APPRECIATION

Deuteronomy 34

The addresses found in Deuteronomy form the basis of the exhortations of Jeremiah and Ezekiel. The New Testament quotes it liberally. Jesus paid special honor to Deuteronomy in the temptation scene (Matt. 4), all three quotations of Scripture which he used to vanquish the Devil being taken from it. (8:3; 6:16; and 10:20). Moses died on Mount Nebo in company with God alone. No man knows his grave to this day. The high tribute given him by the author of the conclusion (34:10-12) proclaims him as the greatest of God's prophets.

THE HISTORICAL BOOKS

JOSHUA through ESTHER

W. A. BENFIELD, Jr.

THE HISTORICAL BOOKS

THE HISTORICAL BOOKS

I. The Gates of Promise

Joshua 1—12
Judges 1

When Moses stood on top of Mount Pisgah and viewed the valley of the Jordan and the cities (especially Jericho) to the east of the river, he was looking upon the land that represented the fulfillment of an age-old promise of Jehovah. This promise was first made to Abraham, then to his children and to their children. It was toward the fulfillment of that promise that Moses' own life had been given to the leading of his fellow men from the bondage of Egyptian slavery. And now, with his own life spent and a new leader appointed for his people, he was privileged to gaze in those last few moments upon the actual gates of promise.

Joshua, the New Leader. For a brief review of the life of the man who was chosen to lead God's people into the Promised Land, read the Westminster Bible dictionary article on Joshua. Study also the biblical references to his earlier life, especially his relationship with Moses, as given in the introductory section of the Dummelow commentary. While little is given regarding Joshua's qualifications for leadership, a heavy emphasis is placed upon the fact that he was chosen by Jehovah and promised divine guidance.

Preparatory Events. (Joshua 1—5.) When Joshua assumed command of the Israelites they were encamped on the east side of the Jordan River at Shittim, a town in the valley between Mount Pisgah and the river. His first task, therefore, was to get his people across the Jordan. After having sent out two men to spy upon the land on the other side of the river, the crossing was made. This miracle of the Jordan, the first endeavor of the people under the new leader, is indicative of the blessings which Jehovah was to shower upon Joshua. As a memorial to the miraculous help of Jehovah, twelve stones from the middle of the Jordan were set up at Gilgal.

The Conquest in Three Campaigns. In order to get a vivid picture of the conquest, a map of Palestine (such as is found in the Bible or Bible dictionary) should be studied carefully. It will be remembered that the territory lying east of the Jordan had been conquered during the lifetime of Moses. This land was assigned to the tribes of Reuben, Gad, and one-half of Manasseh, with the understanding that the people of these tribes were to assist their fellow tribesmen before settling down in their own land. The conquest of Western Palestine may be divided into three campaigns.

1. CENTRAL CANAAN (Joshua 5—9)

The first city which God's people encountered in their march through the gates of promise was Jericho. Like many of the cities of that time, it was enclosed by a wall. The battle strategy which Joshua received in a vision was for the people to march around the city walls for six days, with priests bearing the Ark of the Covenant, and seven other priests going in front of the Ark, blowing silver trumpets. On the seventh day, when the trumpets sounded a long blast, all the people were to shout and the walls of the city would fall down. This was done as commanded, and on the seventh day, when the signal came, "the people shouted with a great shout, and the wall fell down flat, so that the people went up into the city, every man straight before him, and they took the city."

Nearby were the cities of Ai and Bethel, and in the conquest of Ai a different strategy was used. Some among the few thousands first sent against the city were slaughtered, and the rest were routed. Achan had committed sin in keeping a devoted article (see Dummelow), and after this trespass was discovered and punished, the people of Ai were defeated and slain.

Another group of people living in this area were the Gibeonites. Fearful for their lives, after having heard of what had happened to Jericho and Ai, they came to the Israelites, pretending to be a people from a far country, and made a treaty with them. When the deception was discovered, the Gibeonites were made servants of the Israelites.

2. SOUTHERN CANAAN (Joshua 10)

Gibeon was a mighty city, and when the king of Jerusalem heard that it had made peace with Israel, he sent for the kings of surrounding cities and they joined in battle against the Gibeonites. Because of their treaty with Israel, the Gibeonites sent to Joshua for help. The five kings were killed and their cities overrun, which meant that much of Southern Judah was conquered.

3. NORTHERN CANAAN (Joshua 11)
Though there were no modern lines of communication, it did not take the surrounding peoples long to learn of the might of these invading Hebrews. Fearful for their safety, Jabin, king of Hazor, evidently a leader of the people of Northern Palestine, and other kings joined forces to fight Israel. These kings and their people were also delivered over to Israel and the land conquered.

Summary. In studying these first twelve chapters of the book of Joshua, special attention should be given to the writer's emphasis upon the relation of Jehovah to the history of Israel. It has been seen in previous books of the Old Testament; it is evidenced again and again in these chapters. It was Jehovah who gave the battle strategy at Jericho; in the case of every victory of the Israelities, it was Jehovah who delivered the enemy into the hand of Israel.

II. THE NEW HOME

Joshua 13—24

After chapter 12 nothing more is said in the book of Joshua about the conquest of Canaan, except for brief references to the fact that there remained "yet very much land to be possessed." The remainder of the book is given over to an account of the division of the land among the twelve tribes of Israel and to the closing addresses by Joshua. In order to appreciate the conditions under which the Israelites settled down in their new home, the following factors must be considered in studying these chapters.

Canaan a Land of Small Kingdoms. It will have been recognized in the study of the first twelve chapters of this book that Canaan was, at the time of the entrance of the Israelites, made up of many kinds of people and many different kings. The land was not under the rule of one or two groups of people but nearly every large city had its king, though a king sometimes ruled more than one town. Canaan had for the most part been under the dominance of Egypt, and many of the kings of Canaan had been vassals. Letters, known as the Tell el-Amarna letters, have been discovered in which one of the vassal kings of Southern Canaan wrote to the king of Egypt, telling him of the invasion of the land by a group of people known as the Habiru, and asking for help in repelling them. While these Habiru cannot with any certainty be identified as the Israelites, the records do show that by this time the power of Egypt was spent and their vassal kings in Canaan received no help.

The People of Canaan. Someone has said that the settlement of the Israelites in Canaan marked for them an advance in civilization and a decline in religion. The truth of this statement will be seen in a study of the people with whom the Israelites were to associate in their new home. The Canaanites were more advanced in the arts of civilization than were the Israelites who had just come up from the bondage of Egypt and the life of the wilderness. These natives of Palestine were masters of the vocation which naturally resulted from the potentialities of the land, that of agriculture. The Hebrews, on the contrary, had been slaves for many years in Egypt and more lately nomads, wandering in the desert, and were to learn much from their neighbors.

There was also an important difference between the people of Canaan and the Israelites with regard to religion. Much is known today of the religion of Canaan at the time of the entrance of Israel into that land. The spade of the archaeologist has uncovered sanctuaries with their altars, numerous images of Canaanite gods, and other cult objects; even some of the literature of early Canaanite religion has been uncovered. This religion of Baalism should be studied carefully in dictionary articles, as it plays a prominent part in the future of Israel.

The Division of the Land. As will be seen by a study of chapters 13—24, the land of Palestine to the west of the Jordan was occupied by the tribes of Israel in three distinct areas. This division should be studied carefully with the aid of a map. Notice that each of these areas was separated geographically from the others by chains of Canaanite cities that had not been conquered.

The southern part of Palestine was taken by Judah and Simeon. These two tribes were cut off from the others by the Judean hill country and by a line of Canaanite cities along their northern border, such as Gezer and Aijalon.

Ephraim, Manasseh, Benjamin, and Dan occupied the central territory of Palestine. These tribes were separated from the southern tribes by the above-mentioned cities. To the north of these centrally located tribes were the Canaanite cities such as Dor, Megiddo, Taanach, and Beth-shean. These cities formed a barrier between the central tribes and those tribes which occupied the northern territory. These were Issachar, Zebulun, Asher, and Naphtali.

II. PERIOD OF THE JUDGES

Judges 2—21
Ruth

"In those days there was no king in Israel: every man did that which was right in his own eyes."—Judges 17:6

Before his death Joshua sent the children of Israel to possess their inheritance in the land of Canaan. This did not mean, however, that the period of warfare was over and that the Israelites could give themselves wholly to the tasks of a life void of the demands of war. And while each tribe received as its inheritance a certain portion of the land, this did not mean that there would be no future relationships between the tribes.

The Cycle of Events. It has been seen that during the long journey from Egypt and during the conquest of parts of the land of Canaan the Israelites were under the leadership of a man appointed by Jehovah. First it was Moses, then Joshua. But when Joshua died (Judges 2:8) no one was appointed to continue in his place of leadership. And when the tribes possessed the various parts of the land assigned to them (see map) they were so separated by geographical barriers, and perhaps also by family loyalties, that no central form of government was established. Tribal and sectional isolation was the rule of the day.

Separated as they were from other tribes and living so closely with people of Canaan who had not been driven out during the conquest, it was only natural that the Israelites would develop relationships with these neighboring peoples. And in these relationships "the children of Israel did that which was evil in the sight of the LORD." They turned away from Jehovah and worshiped the gods of their neighbors. These relationships became so close that there was inter-marriage between the Israelites and their neighbors. The consequence was that having lost their identity as a separate people, called apart to serve Jehovah, and having gone after other gods, the Israelites became subject to the surrounding nations. In this condition the children of Jehovah pleaded for deliverance and Jehovah "raised up a saviour to the children of Israel." Under the leadership of one after another such "saviour" or judge, the yoke of bondage would be broken and the Israelites freed. Following this deliverance the land would have rest for a period (for example, see 3:30), which meant that the Israelites were free from subjugation for a while and that they did what was right in the sight of Jehovah.

This is what happened over and over again in the period of the judges and is what may be called the cycle of the judges—forsaking Jehovah, social and moral disintegration, subjugation by surrounding peoples, raising up by Jehovah of a judge who rallied the people to break away from their persecutors, a period of righteous living, then religious corruption, subjugation, another judge, deliverance, etc. For a more detailed discussion of these events read the Bible dictionary article.

The Judges. This period of the judges, wherein the people of Israel continued in this cycle of events, is previewed in Judges 2:11—3:6. The remaining part of the book contains a description of these cycles. It is impossible to determine the exact amount of time covered during this period. A chronology of the book may be worked out so as to equal a period of four hundred years, but it may be that more than one judge lived at the same time. Indeed, it seems that the writer, in selecting the stories for the book, fashioned his pattern after a geographical scheme. Deborah and Barak (ch. 4), for example, represent the struggle of some of the northern tribes, Zebulun and

Naphtali, against the Canaanites. Gideon, who led the battle against the Midianites (chs. 6—8), represents the central tribe of Manasseh, which received help from the north. Othniel delivered the Israelites east of Jordan from the Arameans, and Shamgar the southwest tribes from the Philistines.

It was seldom that more than two or three tribes united to fight against their subjugators. It should also be recognized that not all of the persons mentioned in the book of Judges were tribal or national leaders. This is especially true of Samson. He led no rising, gathered no army. He did not attack the foe as the champion and deliverer, and even in his prayer for renewal of strength he thinks only of being avenged on the Philistines for his two eyes.

The Book of Ruth. For the place of the book in the history of Israel see the Westminster Bible dictionary or the introduction to the book in Dummelow. The book is known and loved for its beautiful love story, and Ruth takes a place of importance as an ancestor of our Lord. (See Matt. 1:5; Luke 3:31-32.) Someone has said that after all the scenes of violence and bloodshed which fill the books of Joshua and Judges, the book of Ruth comes in its simple repose like a restful pause. It is one of the most delightful stories ever written; it also helps counteract narrow Jewish nationalism, since Ruth was a Moabitess.

Summary. The period of the Judges reveals clearly the fact that the Israelites had not conquered the people of Palestine. More than this, the period is a warning of the tragic effect that these and other surrounding nations were to have upon God's chosen race. The utter dependence of Israel on Jehovah is also to be noted in the struggles of this period.

IV. Foundation of the Monarchy

I Samuel 1—12

Close of the Period of Judges. The first seven chapters of the book of I Samuel are often identified with the book of Judges because they bring to a close that period of the history of the Israelites. Samuel was the last of the judges of Israel. When he was serving in the house of the priest Eli, the Israelites were defeated in battle by the Philistines and the sacred Ark was captured. (I Sam. 4.) During the twenty years that followed there is nothing known about the relationship of the Israelites to the Philistines. All that is said is that "the house of Israel lamented [or was drawn together] after the LORD." (I Sam. 7:2.) At the close of the twenty years, Samuel held a great assembly at Mizpah. Here they poured out water before Jehovah and fasted. While they were worshiping Jehovah, the Philistines came up to battle, and Jehovah smote them. The Philistines were subdued for a long period and the cities which they had captured were restored to Israel. During this period of peace which followed, Samuel served as what has been called the first circuit judge. He traveled to Bethel, Gilgal, Mizpah, and returned to Ramah.

Preparation for the Monarchy. Samuel must be studied, however, as more than the last of the judges. Samuel was a man of God and as such is often thought of as a prophet. He was perhaps a seer of that old type which had for a long time existed among the Israelites. Dedicated to God before birth and brought by his mother to the home of the priest to live, Samuel profited from all of the good qualities of Eli's house and was left untouched by the evil atmosphere created by the conduct of Eli's two sons.

Samuel's growth in godly character is best illustrated in the visions through which he received revelation from Jehovah. The best-known is that one (ch. 3) through which Eli was warned of the disaster that was to befall his household. After Eli and his sons died, as a consequence of the battle of Aphek, Samuel not only acted as a judge but also ministered unto his people as a man of God. It was during such a service as this that the Philistines made their attack upon the Israelites. (7:5-11.) And it was to this man of God that the Israelites came with their request for a king.

Demand for a King. When Samuel grew old he made his sons judges over Israel. (8:1.) But the sons did not follow after their father; they were dishonest and unjust. Therefore, the people of Israel came to Samuel and asked him to appoint a king over them. (8:5.) The reasons for such a request could be many. Perhaps the memory of Eli's wicked sons was still too vivid in their minds.

Unquestionably the Israelites were influenced by the example of their neighbors, all of whom had their kings. The Israelites had been disunited a long time and the national distress must have weighed upon their hearts. The neighboring peoples had taught them to recognize the advantages which are secured by the consolidation of families and tribes into a kingdom.

The Anointment of Saul. Samuel did not think the request for a king was a wise one. And in answer to his prayer to Jehovah it was revealed to him that such a request did not agree with Jehovah's plan for his people. (8:7-18.) But the people would not listen, and Samuel was instructed to select the king. Having come to know Saul, the son of Kish, a Benjamite of the town of Gibeah, a man of gigantic form and swift, enthusiastic nature, Samuel chose him, under the guidance of Jehovah, to become king over Israel. (Ch. 9.)

Shortly after his selection Saul had opportunity to prove his ability. The city of Jabesh in Gilead was beseiged by the Ammonites. Word was brought to Saul as he was returning with a yoke of oxen from the field. Saul cut his cattle in pieces, sent them in all directions with the threat that so should it be done with oxen of everyone who should refuse to help in relieving Jabesh. The people obeyed the summons, fell suddenly one morning upon the Ammonites, and delivered the beleaguered city. (11:1-11.)

Having thus found Saul the man for their need, the people refused to let him go. In Gilgal, perhaps Joshua's old camp, they made him king. (11:12-15.)

Summary. The establishment of the monarchy is another landmark on the tragic road of the Israelites. In their demand for a king the Israelites rejected Jehovah who, according to the covenant relation of Sinai, was to reign over them. This covenant relationship might have been continued under the kingdom period, but such was not the case. Saul's function as a king was a militaristic one. The internal affairs of the country were permitted to remain as they had been before his accession. War was at once the business and the resource of the new kingdom.

V. THE UNITED KINGDOM

I Samuel 13—31
II Samuel 1—6

Saul's campaign of war was directed for the most part against the Philistines, though it was as a result of his disobedience while fighting the Amalekites (ch. 15) that he was rejected by Jehovah. Samuel was then sent to Bethlehem to anoint the young man David to be king. Again is seen the interpretation of the history of Israel in terms of the guidance of God, for it was Jehovah who directed Samuel in the selection of David, the son of Jesse. (16:1-13.) Though he was but a youth, an occasion presented itself immediately wherein David exhibited the qualities of leadership. This was the well-known experience in which he slew the giant, Goliath, during one of the battles with the Philistines. (Ch. 17.)

Saul and David. The experience of David at the camp of the Israelites brought him into contact with King Saul, and the remainder of the book of I Samuel (18—31) is concerned with this relationship.

There are several things to be noted in a study of these chapters: (1) The merciless persecution of David by Saul, prompted by jealousy and Saul's unbalanced personality. David soon became a favorite of the people, and the jealousy of Saul must be viewed in light of the fact that at that time the king was always expected to be the best man. (2) The grace with which David suffered the results of Saul's hatred. Notice especially the occasion in chapter 26 when David spares Saul's life. (3) The friendship of David and Jonathan. In view of the enmity between David and Jonathan's father, this is one of the most inspiring relationships in history. The familiar story is found in chapters 18:1-5; 19:1-7; 20:1-42; 23:15-18 and in David's lament at the death of his friend as found in the first chapter of II Samuel. (4) The division of the land and the people. The land of Palestine was far from being conquered, even after all these years of occupation. Saul's endeavors to kill David were sandwiched between the Philistine raids. The people were divided in their allegiance. Many were loyal to King Saul and some tried to betray David to him (the Ziphites, ch. 26). David also had a band of loyal men. (5) The death of Saul. The life of Saul came to a tragic climax in the battle with the Philistines in chapter 31. Defeated in battle, his kingdom to be taken away from him because of his godless life, he fell upon his own sword and thus the first king of Israel died.

The Kingdom United. (II Samuel 1—6.) Though he had been anointed previously by Samuel as king of God's chosen people, David had to wait some years for his throne. Even after the death of Saul it was seven and a half years before David became king over all Israel.

After Saul's death David was directed by God to go to Hebron (II Sam. 2), and there he was anointed king over the tribe of Judah. But Ishbosheth, a son of Saul, was made king over the other tribes of Israel, and there followed a war between the two kings. David became stronger and the son of Saul became weaker. The house of Saul was betrayed by Abner, the captain of the hosts (see ch. 3), and was defeated. Then the tribes came to David at Hebron and pledged allegiance to him, and David was made king over all of Israel. (5:1-3.)

But the kingdom was not yet fully united. Jerusalem was still in the hands of the Jebusites, and the Philistines were still the arch enemies of the Israelites. David captured Jerusalem and set up his capital there. When the Philistines heard that he was made king over all Israel they came out to fight against him. The Philistines were defeated in battle (ch. 5), and the Ark was brought to Jerusalem (ch. 6), where David was to reign for 33 years.

The Books of Chronicles. Much of the material of Samuel and Kings is also found in the books of the Chronicles. Read the Bible dictionary article and the introduction in the commentary for a discussion of the relationship of these materials.

VI. THE KINGDOM DIVIDED

II Samuel 7—24
I Kings 1—15
I Chronicles 17—II Chronicles 12

After having been hailed as king of all Israel and having established the new capital at Jerusalem, it appeared as if David's reign would exceed the highest anticipations for the kingdom. One of his great ambitions was to erect a house for the worship of God. This was forbidden him, but he was given the promise that his son should build it. (Ch. 7.)

David brought under subjection the Philistines who for so long a time had been a thorn in the side of the Israelites. The victory over the Philistines (ch. 8) was followed by victories over other nations, including the Moabites, Syrians, Ammonites, and Edomites. Garrisons of men were established in these lands, and such outposts secured the boundaries of the Israelites.

This, then, was the picture in the early days of the reign of David over all of Israel. For the first time since they set foot on the Promised Land under the leadership of Joshua, the Israelites could be content that the land was conquered, that her enemies were subdued. More than this, the people were under the leadership of one man. After many long years of sectional and tribal isolation all the tribes were united under the king. Great, indeed, should be the history of Israel!

Added to this promising picture is David's deed in relation to the family of Saul. (II Sam. 9.) The kind treatment of the crippled Mephibosheth (Merib-baal), son of Jonathan, could only result in good, whether the action was prompted by David's gracious spirit or in the hope of offsetting the silent indignation of the Israelites after the slaughter of Saul's sons.

Seeds of Disunity. But in the long chapters that follow (II Sam. 10—24) little is indicated to fulfill the promise of the growth of the newly formed kingdom. Rather, the seeds of disunity are sown. Chapters 10—12 deal with the successful war against the Ammonites, during which David committed his sin in the case of Bathsheba and Uriah. Following this is a family scandal in which Amnon, son of

David, violated the virginity of his half-sister, Tamar, and was killed by servants of another son of David, Absalom. (Ch. 13.)

This episode served to introduce the rebellion of Absalom and its aftermath, which occupies chapters 15—24. Absalom's murder of his brother could not be overlooked even by an indulgent parent, so he had to go into exile. (13:37-39; 14:21-24, 28.) David thus alienated his son. Absalom's anger at this treatment, and the resentment on the part of many of the people because the capital had been moved from Hebron to Jerusalem, led Absalom to rebel and to set up a new kingdom at Hebron. Absalom's army was eventually defeated and Absalom killed. David mourned the death of his favorite son (18:33), and well he might have mourned also for the future death of his united kingdom. For soon after this rebellion a quarrel broke out between the Judeans and the Israelites. The revolt was put down (ch. 20), but the seeds of disunity had been sown, seeds which were to result eventually in the division of the kingdom.

King Solomon. Adonijah was the logical choice to succeed David as king, but through the help of the prophet Nathan and others, David's wish was carried out and the kingdom was given to Solomon, another son of David. (I Kings 1:5-53.) The history of Solomon's activities as king centers around the building of his palace (7:1-12) and of the Temple which David had wanted to build (chs. 6—8). See the Bible dictionary for a description of the Temple.

One of the principal topics in the biography of Solomon is his wisdom. Promised to him by God in a dream (3:4-15), this wisdom is first manifested in his decision regarding the true mother of an infant (3:16-28). Other passages which relate to his wisdom are 5:12; 10:1-10, 23.

Having been promised a reign of peace, Solomon entered into diplomatic relations with the neighboring kingdoms. He married a daughter of Pharaoh, king of Egypt. (3:1.) He engaged in many business transactions with Hiram, king of Tyre. Acting in the role of an "international middleman," Solomon brought fabulous wealth to his land. The magnificence of the buildings constructed in Jerusalem was due to the development of commerce which made it possible to import materials.

Solomon's wealth was increased by his system of taxation, which brought him 666 gold talents yearly, or more than twenty million dollars. (10:14.) But his diplomatic relationships and his great wealth did not benefit his countrymen. Not only were the people heavily taxed, but some of them were put to forced labor. (11:26-28.) Jehovah was forsaken, the covenant relationship broken. Idolatry was practiced. And out of this situation of social and moral corruption a labor foreman seized an opportunity to revolt, with the result that the kingdom was soon divided.

The Division. Jeroboam was one of Solomon's labor foremen (11: 28), but when Solomon heard of Ahijah's prophecy concerning Jeroboam's future he sought to kill him and Jeroboam had to flee to Egypt (11:29-40). When the king died and his son, Rehoboam, reigned in his place (11:43), Jeroboam returned from Egypt and with a delegation of the people went to the new king to ask that the heavy yoke be removed. Although his wise counselors advised him to heed the request, King Rehoboam refused and added that he would make the yoke even heavier. (12:1-15.)

This, of course, brought about a rebellion. The taskmaster sent by Rehoboam to supervise the forced labor in the north was stoned to death. (12:18.) Jeroboam, who had served as a foreman under Solomon, was made king over the northern tribes. (12:20.) Thus the kingdom, established after years and years of sweat and blood, was divided.

VII. The Northern Kingdom

I Kings 12:1—22:53
II Kings 1:1—17:41

It will be noticed that much of the biblical material for this and the following section is the same. This is because the author of the book mentions every king of the divided kingdoms, Israel and Judah, in chronological order. And instead of finishing the series of rulers of one kingdom before taking up the other series, he shuttles back and forth between the two.

A Bad Beginning. The Northern Kingdom got off to a bad start.

Five kings ruled over the kingdom within a period of forty-five years. Nothing constructive is said about the reign of Jeroboam other than that he fortified Shechem. His son, Nadab, was assassinated after ruling two years. He was followed by General Baasha's reign of twenty-four years during which Israel was at war with Judah. His son, Elah, was also assassinated, and his successor ruled but seven days.

During these years of political corruption the kingdom had lost ground to its neighbors, particularly Moab and Syria. Except in the realm of morals Omri gave Israel a national lift. During his reign the Syrians were held in check, the Moabites were subdued; the capitol was changed to Samaria; more friendly relations with Judah were introduced. Omri's son, Ahab, continued in his father's steps. Syria was soundly defeated. Syria and Israel united to postpone the threat of the rising power of Assyria, but Assyrian inscriptions tell us that they were defeated at the battle of Karkar.

Baalism. When the Israelites first came into Canaan, they came into contact with the cult of the native agriculturists, Baalism. (See the Bible dictionary article.) This relationship of idolatrous worship reached a climax in the reign of Ahab. His Phoenician wife, Jezebel, was a missionary and sought to replace the worship of Jehovah with Baalism.

The sins of which the Israelites were guilty were not only of a religious nature but social as well, as the ideals of Baalism took expression in drunkenness and prostitution. In the midst of this condition there arose two prophets of Jehovah to champion his cause. They were Elijah and Elisha. Elijah's work reached a climax in the contest on Mount Carmel. (I Kings 18.)

Baalism had also reached into Judah through Jezebel's daughter, Athaliah. The contest between Jehovah and Baal came to a head when Jehu, a general in the army of Israel, was anointed king and instructed to destroy the house of Ahab. Jehoram was slain along with Ahaziah, king of Judah. Jezebel was hurled out of a window and seventy "sons" of Ahab were beheaded. (II Kings 9:1—10:7.)

But this systematic religious persecution did not destroy Baalism, as is witnessed in the preaching of later prophets, and the effect on

Israel politically was disastrous. The kingdom was weakened and became prey to the neighboring nations. Syria took land from Israel and under the reign of Jehu's successor, Jehoahaz, reduced it to a mere dependency.

The Golden Age. King Jehoash helped restore the prestige of the kingdom when he defeated Ben-hadad, king of Syria, three times and recovered the cities that had been taken from Israel during the reign of Jehoahaz. (II Kings 13:25.)

Jeroboam II, who followed Jehoash, ruled forty years and it was during his reign that the Northern Kingdom attained the height of its political prosperity. The same was true in Judah under the rulership of Uzziah. Jeroboam II "restored the border of Israel from the entrance of Hamath unto the sea of Arabah." (II Kings 14:25.) Not only were the political boundaries of the country made secure, but the people reached new levels in their economic and social living. This was true, however, in a bad sense. For new wealth led to excesses of luxury, arrogance and pride, oppression of the poor, licentiousness and immorality. These conditions are clearly described and severely condemned in the writings of the eighth-century prophets, Amos and Hosea, who lived in this Golden Age of the Israelites.

Political Decline. The period that followed the death of Jeroboam II was one of increasing internal broils and bloody revolutions. Zechariah, Jeroboam's son, reigned only six months before he was assassinated by Shallum. He in turn was assassinated by Menahem after a reign of one month. It was during the reign of Menahem that the kingdom became involved with Assyria, which was a contributing factor in the final ruin of Israel.

Israel became a vassal of Assyria under Menahem. His son, Pekahiah, ruled but two years before being put to death by Pekah. Pekah joined a coalition, including Rezin of Damascus, to resist Assyria. Judah refused to join the coalition and while Pekah and Rezin were attempting to force King Ahaz of Judah to join the alliance, the Assyrian king defeated the Syrians and the Israelites.

The End of the Kingdom. Tiglath-pileser's subjugation of the Northern Kingdom was the beginning of the end for Israel. It was reduced to a mere province of Samaria and was under heavy tribute. When Shalmaneser succeeded Tiglath-pileser on the throne of Assyria, the Israelites rebelled under the leadership of Hoshea. This, of course, brought Shalmaneser to the scene of the rebellion. Samaria offered desperate resistance, though Hoshea was taken captive, and the nation succumbed only to Sargon, Shalmaneser's successor, in 721 B.C. (II Kings 17:6.) The remaining people were carried away captive and nothing more is known of these exiled Israelites.

VIII. THE SOUTHERN KINGDOM

I Kings 12:1—22:53
II Kings 1:1—23:25
II Chronicles 10:1—35:19

Judah and Israel. When the kingdom of Israel was divided at the death of King Solomon, the small kingdom of Judah, known as the Southern Kingdom, took a position in the background. King Rehoboam, from whom the ten tribes had been taken, prepared to fight against Israel, but was forbidden by the word of the Lord to Shemaiah. The enmity which had existed in the division of the kingdom found expression in the form of fighting under Rehoboam's son, Abijah. The two kingdoms continued to fight until the reign of Asa in Judah and the establishment of the dynasty of Omri in Israel. And when the original enmity was changed into a so-called friendship, Judah found itself drawn into the train of the more powerful neighboring state.

A study of the Scripture references will show that during the reign of the first nine kings of Judah, the experiences of the kingdom were rather normal. Judah was much safer from foreign foes than Israel. Although the Judeans paid tribute to the Egyptians during the reign of Rehoboam, Egypt, as a rule, was not a dangerous enemy. Joash (Jehoash) warded off a struggle with the Syrians by sending the king treasures from the Temple and the palace. (II Kings 12:17-18.)

The history of the Southern Kingdom is also to be characterized by a greater degree of stability in its dynasty. The prominence of the Davidic dynasty lent a measure of permanence to the other institutions of the monarchy, and life in Judah was a much more stable affair, though perhaps not so exciting or dramatic as life in Israel.

The Reign of Uzziah. The first outstanding period in the history of the Southern Kingdom came with the fifty-two-year reign of Uzziah. His reign corresponds with the reign of Jeroboam II in Israel and was equally as outstanding, though little space is given to it in the book of Kings. The fuller account is found in II Chronicles 26. This was a period to be called "The Golden Age" in Judah also, for politically, economically, and socially the kingdom prospered.

Just as the great prophets of Israel came upon the stage during the Golden Age in Israel, so did the same period of prosperity mark the rise of great prophets in Judah. These were Isaiah and Micah. According to Isaiah 1:1 and 6:1, he began his prophetic career in the year of Uzziah's death and continued to prophesy in Judah during the strategic days of the reigns of Ahaz and Hezekiah.

The Kingdom Threatened. After the peaceful and prosperous reign of Uzziah, Judah was plunged into international affairs which ultimately led to its downfall. Uzziah's son, Jotham, enjoyed a peaceful reign, but Ahaz came upon the throne to face the threat of Rezin of Syria and Pekah of Israel. Ahaz summoned the Assyrians to his help against the advice of Isaiah, and Judah became a tributary to Assyria.

Isaiah played an important role in the political life of his day, and Isaiah 36—39 must be read for the history of this period. Realizing the stature of Isaiah, one can almost see his influence as Hezekiah came to the throne, succeeding Ahaz. Under Isaiah's influence, Hezekiah began a reform and it is said of him: "He trusted the LORD, the God of Israel; so that after him was none like him among all the kings of Judah, nor among them that were before him." (II Kings 18:5.)

But Hezekiah's reform was interrupted by the threat of Assyria, which had overrun Israel and taken the people captive. The record of the attack of the Assyrians upon Judah, beginning with II Kings 18:13, must be studied in view of a joint proposal by the Babylonians and Judeans to overthrow Assyria. Relations were also established with Egypt in order to secure its support in case of need. When Isaiah heard the story he gave vent to his feelings, declaring the foreign alliances to be a grave mistake.

Sennacherib, king of Assyria, advanced against Hezekiah from the Phoenician coast, and his conquest threw Hezekiah into a state of panic. He offered his submission to the Assyrians, paid a heavy penalty, and was permitted to keep Jerusalem. (II Kings 18:13-16.) But as Sennacherib went on toward Egypt he changed his mind and demanded the surrender of Jerusalem. Here the prophet Isaiah wielded his greatest influence, and in the name of Jehovah he told King Hezekiah to be of good courage and urged that by no means should he surrender. By a great catastrophe the main army of Sennacherib was annihilated on the frontier between Egypt and Palestine, and Jerusalem was saved. (II Kings 19.)

Political and Moral Corruption. The defeat of the Assyrians had no very great effect upon the external affairs of Judah. For in the reign of Hezekiah's son, Manasseh, Judah was again invaded by Assyria, and Manasseh was for a time held captive in Babylon. (II Chron. 33.) Neither did the work of the great prophet Isaiah change internal affairs, for Manesseh was a bad ruler and caused innocent blood to flow like water. The lawlessness of the time and the disregard of moral restraint are clearly seen in the writings of the prophet Micah.

Josiah's Reform. Manasseh's son, Amon, continued in the ways of his father, but with his death a new era for Judah began, the reform of King Josiah. In the eighteenth year of his reign, the Book of the Law was discovered. These were the laws of the covenant relation entered into at Sinai, which in the course of history with its moral corruption had evidently been discarded and lost. But with the discovery the covenant relationship between God and his people was restored. Josiah abolished the idolatrous practices and the high places were destroyed. (II Kings 22:1—23:25.) It was a happy period of external and internal prosperity. Jehovah and Israel once more went hand in hand!

IX. Captivity and Exile

II Kings 23:26—25:30
II Chronicles 35:20—36:23

The destruction of the Southern Kingdom, like that of the Northern Kingdom, is so closely related to the history of the surrounding nations, especially the Babylonians, that one cannot hope to interpret these chapters without an understanding of this historical background. A supplementary study should, therefore, be made of Syrians, Assyrians, Babylonians, and Persians. (See articles under these topics in a Bible dictionary.)

The Destruction of Jerusalem. The future of Judah seemed bright in the latter part of the seventh century B.C., not only because of the reform instituted by Josiah, but also because of the turn of political events. The Assyrian kingdom, which had brought about the downfall of the ten tribes and which had threatened Judah so heavily, was destroyed by the Medes and Chaldeans. The battle of Nineveh marked the end of Assyria's world dominance, but the change of events did not work for the good of Judah. She had given herself too long to the "mad intoxication of leaders who would inevitably bring her to ruin." Jerusalem was to follow in the steps of Samaria.

The reform of Josiah was cut off by his tragic death in the battle of Megiddo. Dummelow suggests that this battle was the result of conflict between Egypt and Judah over the territory of northern Palestine, formerly ruled by Assyria. (See comment on 23:29.) Josiah's wicked son ruled only three months before he was removed from the throne and replaced by another son of Josiah, Eliakim, whose name was changed to Jehoiakim. He became a vassal of Egypt and did that which was evil in the sight of the Lord.

II Kings 24:1 states that Jehoiakim became the subject of the king of Babylon, Nebuchadnezzar (more accurately Nebuchadrezzar). (See Dummelow's comment.) This sudden turn in servitude (from the Egyptians to the Babylonians) is to be explained by the battle of Carchemish (605 B.C.) where the Egyptians were defeated by the Babylonians. The people of Judah had rejoiced in the fall of Nineveh but it meant only a change of subjugation from Assyria to Egypt. Now Judah rejoiced at the results of Carchemish and the routing of the Egyptians. But they were soon undeceived when the prospect began to open on them of simply exchanging the Egyptian for the Babylonian yoke. The power of Babylonia (Chaldea) had been quite unsuspected but now it was found that in them the Assyrians had suddenly returned to life.

Nebuchadrezzar compelled the submission of Jehoiakim and for three years the king paid his tribute. Then he withheld it and the Babylonians raised against Judah several of the smaller nationalities, especially the Edomites. And when Jehoiachin came to the throne of Judah, Nebuchadrezzar appeared before Jerusalem. The city yielded; the more important citizens were carried into exile, among them the young king, and Zedekiah was made king in his place and reigned eleven years, during which wickedness prevailed. In the ninth year, the Judeans revolted from the Babylonian domination. Help was enlisted from Egypt. And this time the Babylonian army came to lay waste the city. Jerusalem was taken, the Temple and the city were destroyed. King Zedekiah was punished cruelly and a large number of the inhabitants of Jerusalem were deported to Babylon. Thus in 586 B.C. the kingdom of Judah came to an end.

When Judah was threatened by the power of Assyria, the prophet Isaiah came forth to proclaim the inviolability of Zion. In these latter days of the kingdom when Babylon threatened and then conquered, another prophet was on the scene—Jeremiah. His life and teachings, pointing to the doctrine of the new covenant written within the heart, must be studied in light of this historical setting.

In Exile. When the people of Judah were taken to the land of the Babylonians, they were not scattered all over the land but were allowed to remain together in families and clans. There are few existing records of what took place during the period of exile. Some of the people probably merged with the surrounding heathenism, but many continued faithful to Jehovah and to Israel. They must have labored under much sadness and depression, some of them groaning under "the wrath of Jehovah" who had rejected his people and cancelled his covenant.

Circumstances in this foreign land made it impossible for the Judeans to maintain their ritual of sacrifices and feasts; they could only observe days of fasting and humiliation. The observance of the Sabbath, however, and the practice of the rite of circumcision acquired much greater importance. And it is out of these meetings on the Sabbath day that the synagogues seem to have come into existence.

Summary. In the past five sections of study the rise and fall of the kingdom period has been traced. To realize fully its significance the period must be placed in the larger setting of the history of the Israelites which began with Abraham. That "father" of the chosen race was called apart that through his descendants God would bless all nations. For that purpose Moses was raised up to lead the children of Abraham from the bondage of Egypt to the promises of the new land. On the way to that promised land the covenant relationship between Jehovah and his people was established. But the period of stay in the Land of Promise did not yield the fulfillment of the promises. Instead of living as a separate people, called apart to serve Jehovah in a unique way and with special tasks, the Israelites joined hands with the surrounding peoples. And in these associations they often became so absorbed in the political, social, economic, and religious traditions of their neighbors that they forgot Jehovah and his mission for them. Thus the tragic stories of the kingdom period and the captivity.

X. THE RETURN TO THE HOMELAND

Ezra
Nehemiah
Esther

The Return. For some forty-eight years the Jews remained as captives in the land of the Babylonians. Then the judgment of Jehovah was realized upon the people who had brought the chosen race into exile. In the year 538 King Cyrus of Persia brought the empire of Babylonia to an end and permitted the exiles to return to their fatherland. This permission was not made use of by all or even by a majority. The number of those who returned is stated at 42,360. (Ezra 2:64.) It is not known whether women and children were included in this figure.

The Homeland. When the exiles returned home they settled in Jerusalem rather than the whole of Judah. Conditions in the homeland were quite different from the time when they or their parents had left. The people of the surrounding nations had come in and occupied the depopulated territory of Judah. The Jewish population that had remained in the country had intermarried. These "half-breeds" were very friendly with the returning exiles, but they met with no reciprocal cordiality, for the children of the captivity had returned a different people. They had lived in a strange land; they had learned the lesson of religious isolation. And for these returning Judeans, not the native of Judah but the man who could trace his descent from the exiles in Babylon was counted as belonging to their community.

The two books of the Bible that give an account of this period of the return to the homeland are Ezra and Nehemiah. The return was not for the purpose of re-establishing the national boundaries of the old kingdom or the formation of a new political power. This was gone forever. The people now formed a religious community based upon the traditions of a national existence that had ceased. Thus it is that so much of the books of Ezra and Nehemiah are concerned with such things as the building of the second Temple and the reconstruction of the Jewish ecclesiastical organization.

Building of the Temple. After the people had adjusted themselves to their new homes they set about to build the Temple. But after the foundation was laid the work was interrupted by some of the enemies of the Jews who obtained under false pretense a decree from King Artaxerxes to stop the work. (Ezra 4.) Incited by the postexile prophets, Haggai and Zechariah, the leaders of the people, Zerubbabel and Jeshua, appealed to the king on the ground of the edict of Cyrus, who had let the people return for the express purpose of building the Temple. Permission was given to continue with the work.

The Religious Community. After the Temple was completed, Ezra came from Babylon to Jerusalem. (See Bible dictionary article on Ezra.) He was a scribe, versed in the law of Moses, and he came to Palestine armed with authority from the Persian king to proceed upon the basis of this law with a reformation of the community. (Ezra 7.)

The first task of Ezra upon reaching the homeland, and the only one mentioned in the book which bears his name, was that of effecting a strict separation between the members of the true Jewish community of Jerusalem and the other inhabitants of the land. (Ezra 10.)

Shortly after this Nehemiah, the cupbearer and favorite of Arta-xerxes, was sent to Palestine to be the Persian governor of Judea. Ne-hemiah is well known for his leadership in building the walls of Jerusalem amid adverse conditions. (Neh. 3—6.) But Nehemiah and Ezra evidently worked together in introducing the law book as the foundation of the religious community and expanding the covenant relationship. (Neh. 8, 13.) This covenant was based upon the five books of Moses, perhaps identical with what we know today as the Pentateuch.

This emphasis upon the Law, introduced at this period, marked the beginning of the emphasis upon the letter of the Law and the religious formalism which was so prevalent among the Jews at the time of Christ. In fact, with Nehemiah is noted clearly the tragic end of the Hebrew period of the Old Testament and the rise of Judaism which prevailed until the Messiah, the King of kings, was born in Bethlehem.

The Book of Esther. One book of the Old Testament which is often associated with this period of exile and return is the book of Esther. For a study of possible dates see the introduction in Dumme-low's commentary. But the book throws little light upon the his-torical or religious conditions of this period. It centers around the character of Esther who was loyal to her king, her people, and her God. The story is beautiful and inspiring. But no mention is made of Jehovah or of the religious conditions of the day. The book seems to have been written with the purpose of glorifying the Jewish race rather than its religion.

THE POETIC BOOKS

JOB ᴛʜʀᴏᴜɢʜ SONG OF SOLOMON

KENNETH J. FOREMAN

THE POETIC BOOKS

THE POETIC BOOKS

I. The Nature of Poetry

Poets, philosophers, and plain people without number have tried to define poetry. The definitions range all the way from simple and inadequate little epigrams like Wordsworth's "Emotion remembered in tranquillity" or Sandburg's "synthesis of hyacinths and biscuits," to ponderous literary definitions such as may be found in encyclopedias.

Without trying to define it, we may look at some of the outstanding *characteristics of poetry* in every land and age. There is so much poetry in the Bible that without some understanding of poetry and some sympathy with the poetic mind, it is not possible fully to understand this part of the Bible.

1. *Emotion.* A purely scientific description is and ought to be unemotional, impersonal. Poetic expression, on the other hand, is emotional; it is intensely personal. Science speaks the language of the head; poetry the language of the heart. (There are exceptions, but they are not the most loved poems.) Compare a catechism's definition of God with the 23rd Psalm. A prose writer might say, "God is the ultimate object of human desire"; but the Psalmist, a poet, cries out, "My soul thirsteth for God, for the living God." (Ps. 42:2.)

2. *Beauty.* Scientific or technical language is not usually beautiful to read or to hear. But poets seek beautiful words, magical phrases. Why do lovers always prefer to say, "I love you," rather than, "I entertain a persistent affection for you," which means the same thing? It is because the first sentence has a gentle, moving loveliness that the second one lacks. So we may expect to find in the poetry of the Bible some of its most beautiful passages. Indeed, the parts of Scripture committed to memory are most often poems.

3. *Imagination.* The keener and livelier your imagination, the better you will understand the poetic books of the Bible. If you have a prosaic mind, you may even be offended, and you surely will be puzzled, by the Bible poets. You must give them even more poetic

license than an American or British poet would be likely to take. If Mr. Burns sings,

"Oh, my luve is like a red, red rose,"

he does not mean that the girl's face is red or that she has thorns or that she is rooted to the spot. All he means is that she has the same kind of effect on him that a red rose has in June. So you must remember that the Bible poets were all Orientals, and Eastern people even in ordinary conversation are more colorful and flowery than we. When one poet says the mountains "skipped like rams" (Ps. 114), or another one sings of God walking on the wings of the wind (Ps. 104), or Deborah says that the stars fought from heaven against Sisera (Judges 5), it is as stupid to say that it is not "really" so as it would be to tell the young lover that his sweetheart is not "really" like a rose. Rob poetry of its metaphors, of its intensely vigorous, imaginative use of language, and you keep it from being poetry at all.

The poetry of the Hebrews, which means the poetry of the Bible, has all the characteristics of poetry in general which have been mentioned, as well as others. But it lacks two traits which we look for in English poetry: one is rhyme, the other is precise rhythm. Occasionally Hebrew poetry will rhyme, but it is almost a coincidence. And while it has a kind of rhythm (indeed, several kinds, which can be distinguished by a trained ear), it does not "scan" like our poetry. The first line of Poe's "The Raven," for example, has precisely the same number of syllables as the second line; every line of a sonnet has ten syllables, no more, no less. No Hebrew poem is as mathematically exact as that. Hence our English translations are very fine; for the Hebrew irregular, unrhyming lines are translated into English irregular, unrhyming lines, while the rhythmical impression is faithfully preserved. English translations of Hebrew poetry come much nearer preserving the flavor of the original than our translations of (say) Latin or French poems.

The outstanding feature of poems in Hebrew and kindred languages is something we do not have, namely *parallelism*. In its simplest form this means that the poem is written in pairs of lines (called distichs); and the second line of each pair echoes in some way the thought of the first. There is a kind of rhyme of ideas, so to speak, instead of a rhyme of words.

The three forms of parallelism easiest to understand are these:

1. *Synonymous,* where the second line says just what the first says, but in other words. For instance:

"The eye of him that seeth me shall behold me no more;
   Thine eyes shall be upon me, but I shall not be." (Job 7:8.)

2. *Antithetic,* where the second line begins with "But—" and states the converse of the first line. For instance:

"The lip of truth shall be established for ever;
   But a lying tongue is but for a moment." (Prov. 12:19.)

3. *Comparative,* where the second line compares a thing, person, or fact with the statement in the first line. For instance:

"Like as a father pitieth his children,
   So the LORD pitieth them that fear him." (Ps. 103:13.)

For Further Study. Read the section on "Hebrew Poetry" in the Introduction to the Psalms (Dummelow, p. 321ff.), and the article on "Poetry" in the Westminster Bible dictionary. Take a familiar Psalm and see how many different parallelisms you can find in it.

II. JOB: THE DRAMA AND THE PROBLEM

The dramatic poem of *Job* is one of the greatest books ever written. It is totally unnecessary to inquire whether Job is or is not a historical character. Perhaps he was; some think that the book sets forth the writer's own experience. Certainly we need not suppose that five men ever sat around and spoke spontaneously in brilliant poetry, any more than we have to believe that the historical characters in Benét's *John Brown's Body* actually spoke as Benét's great epic "quotes" them.

At all events, it has been truly said that Job lives on every street in the world. He is representative of suffering humanity the world around, desperately questioning the terrible *why* of things.

The book is a long dramatic poem, what we now call a problem play. The problem presented is that ancient and perennial one: Why is it that good people suffer? It is not the problem of suffering, as such. We can all see that some suffering is useful. Without the tooth-ache we could not know when the tooth needs attention. Without the pain we should leave our hand on the stove to be burned. And when someone who has done wrong suffers for it, we feel that justice is being done and we do not feel any great regret. Even when we ourselves sin and suffer the consequences, we are disposed to admit, "I had it coming to me." But when a person suffers in a way that does not seem to have any connection with his past acts, when a truly good or innocent person suffers, then we naturally feel there is something wrong somewhere, and we raise the eternal *Why?*

It is this age-old problem which meets the reader of the book of Job. In the prologue we see Job possessed of the two things that all Hebrews felt were signs of God's blessing and were the materials for happiness: wealth and a family. Yet Job was not spoiled by his prosperity; he was a "perfect and upright" man, fearing God and turning away from evil, praying for all his children. After this glimpse of Job we are taken to the court of Jehovah himself, where the "sons of God" come to report their doings. Among them is Satan, not the horns-and-tail monster of medieval story but a vast and evil power. The sinister fact about Satan in this picture is that he can believe good of no one; not of God, still less of Job. When God learns that Satan has been walking through the earth, he asks him if he has noticed Job, that perfect and upright man.

Oh, yes, Satan says airily, he knows Job. But he does not think Job is good. "Doth Job fear God for nought?" he says. According to Satan, God pays Job well. A fine family, great wealth—anyone will be good for such liberal rewards. Let God only cut off Job's pay, as it were, let God destroy the family and the wealth of this man, and God will find out what Satan knows: that Job is not good at all. Robbed of his happiness, "he will renounce thee to thy face."

Now the singular fact comes out that God believes in Job while

Satan does not. God turns Job over to Satan: "Behold, all that he hath is in thy power; only upon himself put not forth thy hand." God believes Job can stand the worst the Devil can do.

Then comes the dramatic series of disasters; war, flame, and whirlwind destroy the wealth and the children of Job. *"They are dead,"* says the last messenger; "and I only am escaped alone to tell thee."

But God was right. Job was truly good, good regardless. And when next Satan came before God, the Lord repeated his question about Job. Satan (always ready to argue) has a ready explanation. Job still has his health; with this he can found another family and another fortune. Let Job's health and strength be destroyed, so that life shall be reduced to nothing but bare existence in the midst of agonizing pain, and God will hear Job renouncing him.

But God's faith in Job still holds. "Behold, he is in thy hand," He says to Satan; "only spare his life." So Job's days and nights are turned into torture, until when Job, who has long kept silence, finally opens his mouth it is to curse the day he was born.

Meanwhile, three old friends of Job have come a long way to be with him. For seven days they all sit in silence upon the ashes. Then it is that Job breaks out in all his bitterness and despair, and his friends try to answer him. Here the poetic part of the book begins. Hour after hour the four men debate, in language that is moving and sublime; but they reach no conclusion. Job cannot convince his friends that he is innocent, they cannot convince him that he is a sinner. They fall into silence at last from sheer weariness, no longer the good friends they had been. Now speaks up the young listener Elihu, "hammering one golden grain of wit into a sheet of infinite platitude." The older men sit in stony indifference, till Elihu's piping voice is drowned in the roar of an electric storm.

Out of the whirlwind and thunder comes the voice of God, ignoring all the others, speaking straight to Job. Midway of God's speaking Job bursts out begging God to stop. But the voice is relentless, and at the end Job bows in deep submission. Then there is an epilogue (out of place to us, but not to the Eastern mind) in which Job has another and more handsome family, and more wealth than ever before.

For Study. Read straight through the book of Job, at one sitting if possible. What is the argument of Job? of his friends? of Elihu? Does God answer their questions?

III. JOB: THE ANSWERS

One may study the book of Job from many angles. One may admire the beauty of its imagery, the subtle characterizations; one may weep over its tragedy and glory in its passages of triumph.

But here we shall pursue only one thought: the different answers to the problem of suffering which are offered in the book of Job. The book is unique in this: it does not answer the question which it raises. More precisely, it suggests more answers than one, and leaves the reader to decide for himself which is best.

1. *"Renounce God, and die."* This is exactly what Satan is hoping and expecting that Job will do, you remember. Job's wife makes this suggestion outright (2:9), though Job rebukes her for it. Some people today have no better answer, no better reaction in suffering than this. They say in effect, "Either God is bad or he does not care. In any case I am done with him." Now Job at times comes perilously near to denouncing God as unjust, but when all is said and done he never renounces God. He has faith enough to feel assured that God can be counted on at last to do what is right. He feels all the time that the trouble is not with God personally, it is only that he, Job, cannot come close enough to him to understand him. (See 9:32; 23:3-9.) The irreligious person (Job's wife) has really no answer to the problem. Indeed, apart from religion suffering is not a problem as it is to a believer in God. Apart from God, suffering is the natural result of living in this kind of universe. It is only the believer in a good God who has the problem of suffering on his mind. Job would rather keep his faith, problems and all, than throw away problems and faith at the same time.

2. *Suffering is always caused by sin.* This is the view of Job's friends, who hammer the idea into Job's head till he is sick of hearing them. At first gently and by insinuation (e. g., chapter 4) and finally by outright accusation (22:5ff.) they insist that since Job is a

great sufferer he must therefore be a great sinner. Job protests vigorously and even bitterly that his sufferings are out of all proportion
to his sins (16:6-17; 31:1-40); but he does not persuade his stubbornly
logical friends.

There is something in this theory, to be sure. Can you think of
cases where sin has brought its own punishment? But can you not
also think of cases in which the suffering of a person was not connected with anything he himself had done? Can you not name even
some cases in which men have suffered not in spite of doing good but
because of their goodness?

3. *Suffering is a result of events out of our sphere altogether.* This
is the suggestion of the prologue. God there says to Satan, "Thou
movedst me against him, to destroy him *without cause.*" (2:3.) In
the light of the New Testament we may not be able to take this
literally; that is, we as Christians cannot believe that Satan could
talk God into doing anything, and we do not believe that God does
anything "without cause." Nevertheless, the suggestion remains, that
human suffering may well be caused by events of which we are
totally ignorant, as Job was ignorant of Satan's challenge to God. It
certainly is true in the human sphere. How many persons have been
killed in war who had less than nothing to do either with the plan-
ning or the waging of it! How many persons suffer because of the
misdoings of some hidden Satan!

4. *Suffering is a test.* This is essentially the view of Elihu. (Chapters 32—37.) Elihu's speeches, by the way, are so windy and weak
that many scholars believe the great poet of Job could never have
written them. (See Dummelow, p. 313.) But perhaps the genius of
the poet-dramatist is not at fault. Elihu speaks as young men do
speak, very full of themselves, quite sure that they have all the
answers, more full of words than ideas. And Elihu's idea (although
the voice from the whirlwind ignores it entirely) has something in
it, too. Suffering *is* a test of character. In our own nation's history,
Lincoln and Lee are notable examples of men whose greatness was
achieved through much suffering.

5. *After this life we can see the pattern more clearly.* Job himself
feels that he will die without knowing the reason for his agonies;

yet now and then he glimpses another life, in which God will prove to be truly his friend, and his ways will be made clear. (19:26-27.)

* * * * * *

The book of Job never does actually answer its own question: Why do good men suffer? Yet it offers us much practical help. (See Dummelow, p. 291, for a fuller discussion.) The Voice from the whirlwind, battering Job with a tornado of unanswerable questions, brings us face to face with the thought that this is a mysterious universe; we are surrounded constantly by innumerable mysteries. We cannot answer the simplest questions about existence. Pain is only *one* of the many insolubles we have to live with. Another thought is this: In the presence of pain, the great thing is not to have an explanation, but an *attitude*. Not, Why must it be? but, How shall I meet it? Job maintained his integrity from beginning to end. He did not give up his faith in God; he did not let down his own standards of character. After all, it is only the sufferers who can appreciate the heart of God.

IV. THE PSALMS: THE WORLD'S GREATEST HYMNBOOK

For half a thousand years Zerubbabel's Temple stood in sun and storm; today sacrifices and priests and Levites, altar and incense and rituals, have all vanished like the Temple itself. There is only one thing left to us from that long-perished shrine, and that promises to be immortal: its *hymnbook*. The book of Psalms was the hymnal of the second Temple. It was the only hymnal Jesus used. It was the hymnbook of the earliest Christians. It has not only come down to us, it has gone into all corners of the world. From the borders of the unbroken ice to the steaming jungles of the Pacific, men and women today read and love and often sing these ancient songs, the hymns that have never died.

The book of Psalms is not the world's oldest hymnal; that distinction belongs to the Hindu Vedas. It is not the world's largest; our own hymnals frequently have two or three times its 150 numbers. But it may well claim to be the world's greatest hymnal. It is loftier in tone; it speaks to more people's hearts; more varied uses have been made of it than of any similar collection of religious poetry in the world.

Consider it as a hymnal. First of all, we find in it, as we might expect, hymns of various sorts. First there are *personal lyrics,* poems which perhaps the writers did not expect to make public but which appealed to others and so were added to the collection. Our "Abide with Me" is an example of a modern hymn of this personal sort; the 23rd Psalm and the 42nd are examples in the Psalter. Then there are *national songs,* such as our "My Country, 'Tis of Thee" and "America, the Beautiful," both of which are not only poetic prayers for the nation, but also reflect something of our country's history. In the book of Psalms numbers 105 and 106, for instance, reflect on the history of Israel, the goodness of God to his people and their ingratitude to him. Psalm 137, for all its bitterness, breathes an intense patriotism, as do Psalm 122 and many others. A third kind of hymn is *liturgical;* that is to say, it is written definitely for the purpose of a public worship service, perhaps even for some definite part of that service. In our modern hymnals "Bread of the World in Mercy Broken" and "Here, O My Lord, I See Thee Face to Face" are liturgical hymns, meant for the Communion service; "Holy, Holy, Holy" is written for an early morning praise service (and should never be sung at night). Psalm 134 is a good example of a liturgical hymn, written for the use of the night-watchers in the Temple. Psalm 136 was evidently intended to be used by a soloist and chorus, or perhaps by antiphonal choirs.

Like all hymnals, the Psalter was of gradual growth. (See Westminster Bible dictionary, "The Psalms," pp. 497-498, for details; also Dummelow, "Introduction" to the Psalms, sections 6-7.) Scholars differ a great deal about details; but there is good reason to believe that some of the Psalms are even older than David; some were written by him, and some were obviously written long after the "Exile" began. Most of them, like so many of our own, are anonymous. The "titles," or ancient notes indicating authorship and circumstances in which the Psalm may have been written, were put in by editors of later times, and are far from reliable. It is only by a careful examination of the content, vocabulary, and thought of a Psalm that one can now reach sound conclusions about its date of composition.

Like a good modern hymnal, too, the present Psalter's hymns were gathered in many cases out of earlier collections. The Bible dictionary names six of these. Naturally, in a compilation, hymns may be duplicated. Thus Psalms 14 and 53 are almost exactly alike. (Can you tell the outstanding difference between these two?) It is evident that this Psalm was a popular one and had been in at least two hymn collections before finding its way into the second Temple's hymnbook. Then hymns may be changed (and even improved!). At the writer's elbow is a little Lutheran hymnal of 1817, which contains some of our most familiar older hymns, but not always with the same wording that we use. So there is considerable evidence of revision in the Psalms, and scholars can often conjecture their original forms. Sometimes hymns are put together in new ways. For example, compare Psalm 40:13-17 with Psalm 70. Either 70 is a shortening (and revision) of 40:13-17, or the writer of Psalm 40 copied in Psalm 70 for an effective ending. Also Psalm 108 is not original at all, verses 1-5 being taken from Psalm 57:7-11, and verses 6-13 from Psalm 60:5-12.

All these things are interesting enough; but what endears the Psalter to us most of all is the fact that our Lord used it, and his religious life was nourished by it. On the last night before the crucifixion we hear of him singing a hymn before going out to Gethsemane. What the hymn was we can be reasonably sure, for on Passover Eve the group of Psalms 113—118 was regularly sung, 113 and 114 early in the meal, and 115—118 after the last cup of wine. If you will read that group of Psalms, trying to think what they must have meant to Jesus on that sad night, they will have a new meaning for you.

For Further Study. See how many Psalms you can classify into one of the three types named above. See end of Bible dictionary article, and headings of the Psalms in Moffatt's translation for hints on the musical accompaniment of the Psalms. Study your own hymnal to see how much use is made of the Psalms today.

V. THE PSALMS: MIRROR OF MAN

John Calvin once called the book of Psalms "the mirror of the soul." And so it is. Dr. William Lyon Phelps said that one can learn more about human nature from reading the Bible than from living in New York. This would be true even if one explored no further than the Psalms. Nothing is more intensely personal than lyric poetry; and in these lyric poems of faith, despair, hope, anger, joy, and grief, we have a many-sided picture of the "well-known human race."

1. *The bad man.* Psalm 1 sets him before us, alongside the good man. He is presented as the exact opposite of the good man. The ungodly, compared with the righteous, are "not so." The bad man does walk in the counsel of the wicked, he stands in the way of sinners, he sits in the seat of the scornful; his delight is in anything but the Law of the Lord. We meet the bad man in nearly every Psalm. In Psalm 2 he is raising a tumult, filled with vain ambitions; in Psalm 3 he is mocking those who trust in God; in Psalm 4 he loves vanity and seeks after falsehood—and so on.

The reasons and the details of his badness are made plain. He is proud (10:4); a fool (14:1); he lives on the toil of others (37:21); he thinks God is like himself (50:21); he is a gangster (55:9ff.); his tongue is a sharp sword (57:4); he is a hypocrite whose mouth is smooth as butter but whose heart is war (55:21); he is willfully deaf (58:4); he encourages himself in an evil purpose (64:5).

The road to wickedness is plotted again and again. As striking a passage as any is in 36:1-4. Badness starts with disregarding God and flattering oneself. The bad man prides himself on "getting away with it" (vs. 2); his talk is foul and false; he has given up being wise and doing good. He lies awake nights thinking up new iniquities; he stubbornly keeps on in the wrong direction; and finally he "abhorreth not evil," his conscience becomes so seared that he no longer shrinks from evil; wrong looks right to him.

Possibly the poets who wrote these Psalms allowed more than a tinge of contempt to color their descriptions; but Christians might do well to cultivate a fastidiousness of character; if we can see evil as it is, contemptible and disgusting, we shall be less tempted by it.

2. *The emotional man*. Poetry, as we know, is the language of emotion; and in many a Psalm we see the excitement and turmoil of minds not at rest. The familiar Psalm 42 portrays the upswing and downswing of a soul tossed between faith and hopelessness; 6:6 might well describe the nights of a sufferer from nervous prostration. The sick man, with all his tremors, his distorted outlook on life, appears again and again (in Psalm 41, for example). Fear of death is expressed in 30:8-9 and 143:7, as in the agonizing 88th Psalm; deep loneliness in 142:4 and 31:11. That most dreadful of all emotions, despair, is given classical expression over and over again. Psalm 88 is one sustained threnody of desperation, without one note of hope. More fleeting yet equally dark glimpses of the shadows in a hopeless soul are seen in 143:3; 89:45-48; 69:1-3; and elsewhere. It was most natural that when Jesus hung forsaken between earth and sky, there came to his lips in the deepest moment of his agony a quotation from one of these ancient Poems of Pain: Psalm 22:1—"My God, my God, why hast thou forsaken me?"

3. *The good man*. The student should take a notebook and go through the Psalter picking out the many traits that make up the well-rounded character of the truly good man.

We see the good man gone wrong, often enough: fretting (37:1), questioning the high justice of God (73:1-16), seeking vengeance and cursing his enemies (35:1-8; 58:10; 69:18-28; 109:6ff.; 137:8-9). But we see also the good man in his better hours. These poets are sinners indeed, but they know true repentance. The "penitential Psalms" are among the best known of the collection: such as 6, 32, 38, 51, 102, 130, 143. The psalmists are not always complaining; the note of joy is often heard (e. g., 97, 100, 144). We find the good man loving his family (127, 128) and his country (105, 106, 125, and many others). We see him at worship and loving the house of God (84, 118); out of doors seeing God's power and goodness in nature (104); helping others, living a life of strength in body and in character (1, 15). Above all, we see the good man coming close to God and finding all the satisfaction of his soul, all his comfort and joy and power, in the "shadow of the wings" of the Almighty God (23, 73, 139, and many others). No psalmist was a perfect man; but the hymns they left behind them demonstrate that even imperfect men may know the perfect God.

VI. The Psalms: The Poets' God

Christians who have been nourished on the Bible and whose religious ideas come mainly from that book probably derive their most comforting and satisfying ideas of God from the poetic parts of Scripture. The Psalms introduce us not to the businessman's God, insisting on his contracts, never giving something for nothing; nor do we meet the professor's God, wrapped in cloudy abstractions. The poets of the Bible offer us no definition of God at all. What they say about God is not prosaic, not philosophical, not even logical. It is in the emotional, vivid language appropriate to poetry. Yet it is always the poets' God who comes closest to the human heart.

1. God is often *described in metaphor*. The student should take notebook and pencil and leaf through the Psalms, with the aid of a commentary, and discover at firsthand what these poets have said about God. In 36:6-9, for instance, there is a cluster of metaphors. God is like the great mountains; he preserves man and beast; his wings overshadow the children of men; he is a generous host (the "fatness of thy house" refers to an abundance of luxury foods); he is a flowing river, a fountain of life, the sun in the sky. To complain that the poet mixes his metaphors is beside the point. He is no doubt aware of doing so. He simply wishes to express the inexpressible abundance and riches of the infinite God, and he piles one figure of speech on another in his attempt to put his feelings into words. In 63:1 God is a cold spring, in 62:6 a rock and a tower; often he is described as with wings (17:8; 36:7; 91:4, for instance). He rides on the sky. (68:33.) One poet is not afraid even to picture God like a "mighty man that shouteth by reason of wine." (78:65.) God is a gardener (80:8ff.); he is the burden-bearer of his people (68:19); he is a shepherd (23), a builder (51:18), a judge (9:4), a king (47), a father (103:13).

2. In these and other ways, certain *great facts about God* emerge.

He is eternal (90:1-2; 102:24-27); the God of all nations and not of the Jew alone (67); he is the Creator (33:6; 89:11) and the true owner of the earth and all that is in it (24:1; 50:10-11). He inspires terror (47:2; 66:5; 68:35); yet he is just, and requires justice in the lives of those who claim to serve him (Pss. 15, 24, 101, 111). And always he is friendly. He shows his friendship to those that fear him (25:14); he is the "God of deliverances" (68:20). The whole 103rd Psalm (one of the best-known favorites) is full of references to the "benefits" of God: He forgives, heals, crowns, satisfies his children.

3. *How God is found.* Among others, we may note four plain ways in which the writers of these ancient hymns have shown us how to find God. First, he may be found in history. Just as our "America, the Beautiful" refers to our own history, and "A Mighty Fortress" reflects the stirring times of the Reformation, so these Hebrew hymns often look back and see how God's hand was in the story of their people. The twins 77—78 and 105—106 are excellent examples of this religious philosophy of history. The psalmists are a long way from contending that everything that happens (good or bad) is God's personal doing; but they do teach that God weaves even the crooked threads of man's evil will into the pattern of his great designs. He makes even the wrath of man to praise him. (76:10.)

Second, God may be found in nature. The idea in the familiar 19th Psalm is found in many other places. Psalm 18:6-17 brings God before us in electric storm and earthquake, in hailstones and coals of fire. The wind is the blast of his nostrils. (18:15.) The 8th Psalm reminds us that in understanding and in controlling nature, man is acting in partnership with the creative God. In the famous Psalm 104 all nature, even in aspects of it we do not ordinarily love, is seen as not only revealing God but as obeying his commands, an expression of his will. The poem ends with lines that remind us of our own hymn, "Where every prospect pleases, and only man is vile." If there is evil in the world it comes from man, not nature! Yet nature is not divine; it is the garment of the invisible Deity, yet God is far above all that he has made (e. g., Ps. 93).

Again, God is found in law, particularly in the inspired law of

Moses. The 119th Psalm, artificial as its structure is (see Dumme-low), is evidence of the love of its author for the law of God. Who-ever wrote that poem (the longest chapter in the Bible) could see God much more clearly in his laws than in nature or in what we would call the church.

Finally, God is to be discovered in personal experience. This is the recurring theme of the entire book of Psalms. Notably he is to be found precisely in those experiences which for some persons seem to dim the reality of God, namely in trouble and distress. Psalm 107, for example, gives five pictures of the presence of death: being lost in a desert, captivity, extreme illness, a shipwreck, and famine; and in each of these trials the singer sees the lovingkindness of God. So through all the experiences of life, the brightest and the blackest, the psalmists cry:

> "In the shadow of thy wings will I rejoice. . . .
> Whom have I in heaven but thee?
> And there is none upon earth that I desire besides thee."
>
> (Ps. 63:7; 73:25.)

VII. PROVERBS: WISDOM IN CAPSULES

A governor of Virginia said in recent years that during his term of office he received more help in his problems from the book of Prov-erbs than from any of the books on political and social science with which his bookshelves were provided. Certainly no other book in the Bible is so crammed from end to end with practical advice. No other book is so explicitly intended for use by young people. (1:4.) It is the light of experience for those who need experience. (As who does not?)

In general, the book* consists of three parts: a long poem in praise of wisdom (1—9), a collection of miscellaneous proverbs, strung to-gether with very little if any order (10—27), and a number of short passages dealing with particular themes, ending with the noble poem in praise of the ideal woman (31:10-31). Except in the first and last

---

* For a complete outline of this book, see the Westminster Bible dictionary; for views regarding the authorship, see the Bible dictionary and Dummelow.

parts, which should be read by sections, as printed in the A.S.V., the reader should not attempt to read straight through, as one would read Genesis or Luke. That would be as bad as taking at one time all the pills the doctor ordered. Let the eye skim down the page till it lights on some striking thought: stop with that, *memorize* it, think about it, put it into practice; and then do it again. Proverbs is really the only book in the Bible which can profitably be read by the inch-at-a-time method, for its wisdom is put up in capsules.

This book is a part of what is called the "Wisdom Literature." Four books form this group; two are in our Old Testament. Proverbs and Ecclesiastes, and two are in the Apocrypha, Ecclesiasticus and the Wisdom of Solomon. (Incidently, anyone who likes Proverbs will certainly like Ecclesiasticus, which can be found in any translation of the Apocrypha.) Parts of Job and Psalms also come in this category.

Dr. Easton, in the International Standard Bible Encyclopedia, has pointed out some characteristics of all the Wisdom Literature, wherever found. As you read in Proverbs, check to see whether you do not find all these qualities in the book.

1. God is the source of true wisdom. E.g., "The fear of the LORD is the beginning of wisdom" (9:10); "The LORD possessed me in the beginning of his way" (8:22).

2. True wisdom may be learned everywhere. The seeker for wisdom does not need to find learned men and great books or universities.

> "Go to the ant, thou sluggard;
> Consider her ways, and be wise." (6:6.)

Go out and sit on an ant hill and you will find a professor of wisdom crawling up your leg. Look at the spider, at the serpent, at the ship in the sea; listen to old men talking; you can learn wisdom everywhere if you keep your ears and your mind open.

3. The principal good in life is wisdom. Job 28 is a beautiful passage comparing and contrasting wisdom with all the jewels of the earth. There is no market where you can put down even a king's ransom and say, "Wrap me up a parcel of wisdom." There is noth-

ing else to compare with it. This marks off the Wisdom Literature point of view, for in these books it is not happiness or success, not even goodness or faith that is the main thing, but "Wisdom is the principal thing; therefore get wisdom." (4:7.)

4. Wisdom is often personified. One of the loveliest parts of the long poem which introduces the Proverbs is in chapter 8, where Wisdom invites the sons of men to be her guests. She tells of her early days, when before the earth was made she was the companion and the delight of God.

5. In considering the last two points, we have to remember that we are Christians, and that we cannot regard the viewpoint of the Wisdom Literature as final. For Christians cannot agree to these two features of these books, however heartily we may agree on the others. (See Dummelow, p. 379.) In the Wisdom Literature (including, of course, Proverbs) there are just three classes of persons: the wise, the fool, and the young or immature. The young man can become a wise man or a fool. But once a fool, always a fool. There is no hope of the fool's changing.

> "Though thou shouldest bray a fool in a mortar with a pestle . . .
> Yet will not his foolishness depart from him." (27:22.)

Grind a fool to powder; every grain of him will still be a fool. The idea of *conversion*, which is of the essence of the Christian gospel, the concept of the new birth, does not appear in the Proverbs.

6. The Wisdom Literature is strictly one-worldly, this-worldly, in its outlook. Here and there in the Psalms and once or twice in Job are foregleams of immortality, but not in Proverbs or its kindred writings. The general theme is: Be good and you will prosper; God's rewards are given here on this earth, to men in their lifetime. This was essentially the view of Job's friends, and we have seen how inadequate it is. A wider experience led God's people to a higher view of God's ways with man. After Christ "brought life and immortality to light through the gospel" (II Tim. 1:10) we know that God does not settle all his accounts of this planet *on* this planet.

Nevertheless, as one-worldly wisdom the book of Proverbs is unsurpassed. Wisdom, priceless as ever, still stands at God's right hand.

VIII. Ecclesiastes: The Religion of a Cynic

The book of Ecclesiastes is called poetical only by courtesy. There are a few brief poetical passages in it, as a glance at Moffatt's translation or the Revised Standard Version will show; but for the most part it is a prose essay. Its inclusion in the poetical books may be due to the embarrassment any editor would find in attempting to classify it. For this book is totally unlike any other book in the Bible. Indeed, the reader is likely to be shocked by it repeatedly. The author is evidently someone whose whole view of life and duty and destiny is different from that of other biblical authors.

Nevertheless we may well be glad that the ancient editors of the Bible decided to include this strange book. If the Bible is medicine for the soul, Ecclesiastes may be like strychnine, a poison which is a tonic; dangerous in large doses, but sometimes a lifesaver.

Who the author of Ecclesiastes was we do not know. (See the Bible dictionary and Dummelow for the reasons why Solomon could not have written it.) Whoever he was, he was clearly a cynic, that is to say, a person who has drained the cup of life and found it bitter, or rather has found it altogether empty. "Vanity of vanities" is his verdict on life (1:2)—emptiness of emptiness. He is not a backwoods cynic, he is not someone from the bottom of the heap, angry at life for having passed him by. He is no young man, suffering the disillusionment of youthful disappointment. He is an old man, wealthy and powerful. He has been able to do exactly as he pleased. He has had everything in life—except happiness. Life for him is a "striving after wind"—you cannot catch the wind, and if you did, all you would have would be an armful of nothing.

It is interesting—and appalling—to note the many things which make life worth living for most people, which the old cynic rejects. Of money he says, "He that loveth silver shall not be satisfied with silver." (5:10.) Pleasure and power he counts alike as vanity. (2:1; 4:13-16.) The pursuit of novelty is a dreary round. (1:1-11.) Work does no good. (2:20-23.) Of study he finds it a "weariness of the flesh." (12:12.) Indeed, with regard to all learning he would feel sympathetic with the famous (bad) definition of philosophy: a blind man in a dark cellar at midnight looking for a black cat that isn't there. "Reality is beyond my grasp . . . no one can lay hands upon the heart of things." (7:24, Moffatt's translation.) Of love he remarks only that there are times when hatred is more appropriate (3:8), and although he admits having found one true man in a thousand, "a woman among all those have I not found" (7:28). "Youth and the dawn of life are vanity" (11:10), but old age brings no compensations; it is called "the evil days . . . when thou shalt say, I have no pleasure in them" (12:1).

Worst of all, when this ancient cynic stands at the threshold of death he does not have the consolation of seeing a better world, or even any world at all, beyond the grave. Sometimes he doubts (3:21), and at other times he flatly denies, immortality (9:2-6, 10). Nothing but dust and darkness is the end of the road.

The importance of Ecclesiastes is in this: *he does have a religion.* It is not a rich and happy religion. It may be called religion at its lowest terms; but it is real. In our modern age, above all things an age of cynicism and world-weariness, we may often need Ecclesiastes to remind us that even at life's worst it is still possible to keep some religion.

The elements of this cynic's religion are four. First, work for work's sake. Not for reward, not for permanence, but for the sheer joy of labor. (5:18.) Second, enjoyment of the gifts of God. Granted they are tinsel; at least they shine. Take the joy of the passing day as it passes, not demanding that it stay. "Go thy way, eat thy bread with joy, and drink thy wine with a merry heart." (9:7.) "Live joyfully with the wife whom thou lovest." (9:9.) "Let thy heart cheer thee in the days of thy youth, and walk in . . . the sight of thine eyes." (11:9.) Third, sharing the gifts of God. "Give a portion to seven, yea, even unto eight . . ."; "Cast thy bread upon the waters; for thou shalt find it after many days." (11:2, 1.) The banquet of life may be only a crust; yet a crust shared is a sacrament of friendship. And a fourth element in the cynic's religion is belief in God. This ancient man did not know God well. Of God's love he has no inkling at all; of God's grace he feels no need. Nevertheless he says, "Fear God, and keep his commandments." (12:13.) Though everything else fall to pieces about you, it is still right to do right. If you cannot love God at least you can obey him.

This is a cold religion, to be sure. It will not support a Job in his afflictions; nor will it inspire a Paul. Nevertheless it is real. And when in some shipwreck we flounder in the trough of tremendous seas, if we cannot at the moment reach the safe deck of some passing liner we shall not scorn the life preserver that may be thrown within our reach. So in God's providence this strange old cynic's essay has been kept. In life's downswings it may be all to which a man may cling, till at last he sets his foot upon the rock.

IX. THE SONG OF SOLOMON: "LOVE IS STRONG AS DEATH"

The Song of Solomon is another unique book. It comes near not mentioning the name of God at all, and then only once (8:6, A.S.V.) in a phrase that is as little religious as "God-forsaken" is in English. It is the only book in the Bible which is devoted exclusively to the one theme of love—not love in general, but love between man and woman. A poem which begins,

"Let him kiss me with the kisses of his mouth"

and begins its last stanza,

"Make haste, my beloved"

is certainly different from all the other Old Testament poetry we have seen.

A more ascetic age than ours was much embarrassed by this. How could love poetry have a place in the Word of God? But there the poem was, lovely, lilting, passionate, unashamed. So it was thought, once upon a time, that surely the poem could not mean what it said. The Jews adopted it into the Canon (i.e., they accepted it as Scripture) only on the supposition that the love celebrated in this poem does not refer to men and women but to God (the man) and Israel (the woman). When Christians began to see in the Old Testament fore-glimpses of Jesus Christ, their enthusiasm led them in many cases to see prophecies where no prophecies were. This entire book was said to portray the relations between Christ (the man) and the church (the woman). Other interpretations called the poem an allegory of God and the soul; or of the Holy Spirit and the Virgin Mary. But common sense, or perhaps a sense of humor, has convinced most students of this book in our times that we are to see in it precisely what it obviously sets out to be, singularly beautiful poetry, Oriental in its warmth and imagery, describing and praising the love of a woman for a man and of a man for a woman.

In reading it, one must constantly remember that this came from "East of Suez." It is not sensual, but it is sensuous—that is to say, it appeals to the five senses. Taste (2:3), smell (2:13; 4:11-16), and touch (5:2), as well as sight and hearing, all contribute to the almost cloying sweetness of its effect. As compared with similar Eastern poetry, this poem is remarkably restrained and chaste. It is only when it is compared with the product of our chillier climes that it seems to go too far.

One must look out for Oriental metaphors, consulting the commentary for details. No American boy would tell a girl that her hair was like a flock of goats (4:1) or that her teeth looked like sheep (4:2). He would surely not think of telling her (if it were true) that her neck reminded him of a tower of David (rough and immense!), and still less that her nose was like a tower on a mountaintop! (4:4; 7:4.) But a girl of the Near East would feel that these were high compliments.

As for the poem itself, your commentary will explain the various theories that have been developed to interpret it. The headings of the pages in the American Standard Version suggest one of these: namely, that the poem is a dialogue between two persons. You can follow the "plot" by reading the headings straight through. On this theory the plot is simple: Man meets girl, man loses girl, man finds girl, man marries girl. Another, and for a long time the most widely held explanation, was that the poem presents the "eternal triangle" with two men and one girl. Of the men, one is a shepherd lad, and one is King Solomon (that much-married man) himself, wanting to add the shepherd's sweetheart to the royal harem. The girl is tempted —as who would not be? King Solomon's palanquin (3:9-10) far outshines a Cadillac convertible—but finally true love prevails, and the two young lovers are united on the hills of spices in the soft, sweet springtime. (For details of this plot, see the Westminster Bible dictionary, p. 573.)

Whether we take either of these interpretations, or the now commoner one that the "Song of Songs" is what its name implies, a small anthology of love songs, without plot or connection except for the recurring theme, we can safely take it as an inspired poetic tribute to human love.

It is well that a solemn book of religion should contain such a poem, for by it we are reminded that love is of the essence of life—that the renewal of human life on the earth, the carrying out of God's purpose from generation to generation, begins in love stories, even between persons as obscure as the hill peasants of these flowing lyrics. We are reminded of the importance of love, and of its beauty and its permanence. The Song of Songs tells us of love that is altogether different from lust, love that is far other than a passing fancy, love that is interwoven with all the glory and beauty of the world, as well as with the work and play of everyday living. It sings of a love whose whisper is stronger than the trumpetings of a king's splendor; love which alone is strong as death, as undying flame.

> "Many waters cannot quench love,
> Neither can floods drown it:
> If a man would give all the substance of his house for love,
> He would utterly be contemned."

X. LOOKING FOR POETRY IN THE BIBLE

As we have seen, the so-called Poetical Books of the Old Testament are not all poetry. On the other hand, by no means all of the poetry in the Bible is in these books.

There are two ways you can look for poetry in the Bible. One is the simple method of looking for what is *printed* like poetry. The King James translation will give you no help, for at the time of that translation (more than 300 years ago) the nature of Hebrew poetic literature was not understood, and all is printed like prose. The American Standard Version is better, especially in the Old Testament; the Revised Standard Version or one of the other modern translations like Moffatt's is better still. With the aid of these you can skim rapidly through the pages and find numerous poetic passages. Hebrew writers often slip from prose into poetry and back again, even when most of the writing is prose.

Another way of looking for poetry, which calls for more sensitive appreciation, is to notice whether those marks of Hebrew poetry noted in part 1 of this section are to be found. Especially when rhythmical phrases show a marked parallelism, one can suspect a poem.

Some of the noteworthy poetical passages are here indicated. The first person we hear of who used poetic speech was Lamech, in Genesis 4. This does not mean that the author of Genesis implies that poets are bad people! The author himself has already made use of poetry; but the incident may well suggest that art can be and often is used in the service of evil. The beautiful and the good ought to be hand in hand always; too often they are not.

Samson used not poems but rhymed jingles, for his famous riddle. (Judges 14.) A more effective judge, the great woman Deborah, sang a song which has come down to us in Judges 5. We cannot call this a Christian hymn, of course. Its spiritual distance from the New Testament is measured by the fact that the identical praise is given to Jael here (Judges 5:24) that is accorded to the mother of Christ by Elisabeth (Luke 1:42). The vengeful gloating over the sorrow of Sisera's mother is a world removed from the spirit of one who said, "Love your enemies." Nevertheless this ancient poem, genuinely revealing the spirit of those times, is a stirring battle hymn of faith and courage. Deborah might be no Christian saint, but she did have a solid foundation of faith—faith in a God who was on the side of justice and against all oppressors of the world. When read aloud this triumph song of Deborah is one of the most thrilling poems that has survived from ancient times.

There was other war poetry in Israel. In Numbers 21 we have several fragments of a lost collection, "The Book of the Wars of the LORD." Another anthology, now lost except for two quotations, was "The Book of Jashar," evidently a collection of hero poems. A few lines from it are found in Joshua 10 and a whole poem, "The Song of the Bow," in II Samuel 1.

The book of Lamentations is a collection of dirges. It will be noticed that each chapter has 22 verses except chapter 3, which has 3 times 22 or 66. This is because each chapter (except the fifth) is an acrostic: each verse begins with a successive letter of the Hebrew alphabet. In chapter 3, three verses, instead of one, begin with the same letter. No book in the Bible (says Dummelow) shows greater art or more technical skill in composition. Isaiah 14:4-21 is written (in Hebrew) in the same meter as Lamentations, while the 119th Psalm is an 8-fold acrostic.

Passing over the prophetic books, which abound in poetic passages, one may suggest some New Testament poems. Three which are used in our church services have been given names from the first words of their Latin form: the "Magnificat," the "Benedictus," and the "Nunc Dimittis." These are all found in Luke 1 and 2. These may serve to remind us that Jesus came of a poetic family. Add to this fact Jesus' necessary familiarity with the Psalms and other Old Testament poetry, and we are not surprised that Jesus himself used poetic language. A glance through the Revised Standard Version or Moffatt's translation will call your attention to many such passages in Jesus' teaching. The story of Jesus shows how poems cling to the mind. On the very cross, in the deepest of his pain, what came to his lips was not a word of his own but a verse from the 22nd Psalm, "My God, my God, why hast thou forsaken me?" and at the very last, he died with a line from another poem on his lips: "Into thy hand I commend my spirit." (Ps. 31:5.)

At the end of the New Testament, in the book of the "Unveiling," (Revelation) the description of the new heaven and the new earth is largely in poetry. Prose may do justice to earth, but only a poet can write of heaven.

God has set in man's mind the love of beauty, and to some he has given the capacity for creative art. But we are all poets when we read a poem well, as Carlyle said; and in our response to the poetry of the Bible we realize again that truth has added power when beauty serves her well.

THE MAJOR PROPHETS

ISAIAH through DANIEL

E. D. KERR

THE MAJOR PROPHETS

Isaiah

Jeremiah

The Lamentations of Jeremiah

Ezekiel

Daniel

THE MAJOR PROPHETS

"Understandest thou what thou readest?" We may sometimes hear people speak with wistful longing of not understanding the Bible. Their reading, then, is likely to be much neglected and limited to a few familiar passages, or to be a task of comparatively little real delight or spiritual profit.

To the beginner in the study of the Old Testament prophets, or to the discouraged seeker after their hidden treasures, the guidance that is richly available and the suggestions that lead to it will be found exceedingly helpful. A few simple hints may be listed here. Others will suggest themselves or may be found elsewhere.

1. Occasional and fragmentary reading is not likely to lead to much understanding. The reading, in order to be highly fruitful, must be accompanied by serious study.

2. An excellent plan is to study a book at a time. The book may, of course, be divided into sections for convenience of handling. Each section, while not independent of the others or of the whole book, should have a real completeness in itself.

3. In studying a prophet's message it is necessary for the student to become acquainted with the history of the times in which the message was given. The prophets spoke first to their own people, with their particular and immediate duties, problems, perils, and sins. Unless we know the circumstances our understanding of the prophet will be sadly limited.

4. The student may profitably use his imagination, aided by all available knowledge, to make the life and ministry of the ancient prophets real to us today, and to bring down to our times and apply to our circumstances the eternal principles of truth which they taught.

5. It is very important to have reference books at hand and to use them constantly. Dummelow's commentary and the Westminster Bible dictionary have been specifically recommended for use with this volume.

6. Much light and knowledge may be gained from improved modern translations of the Bible, of which a number are on the market.

7. Most important of all is an eagerness to know God's revealed truth, and so to approach the task with a humble, teachable spirit. The goal of the study is the knowledge of God and of his will. "He that cometh to God must believe that he is, and that he is a rewarder of them that seek after him." (Heb. 11:6.)

ISAIAH

Isaiah's prophetic career covered the period 740-700 B.C. Not much is known of his personal life, but the influence of his ministry was very great. In troubled times his testimony held a remnant true to the God of Israel. And that testimony continues to be living and powerful. Isaiah is usually rated as the greatest of the prophets.

Isaiah is often called the statesman prophet. He was in close association with the kings, whether they heeded his counsel or not. It is necessary for the reader who would understand his book to have a sufficient knowledge of the history of the Israelitish kingdoms, the neighboring peoples, and the world powers in the latter half of the eighth century B.C.

The prophets, Isaiah and the others as well, were preachers of righteousness. They were not chiefly engaged in predicting details of future events, near or remote. They saw and predicted glorious coming manifestations of God's righteousness and redemptive work; but the present was always the time for men to walk in the light of the Lord and to do his will. The prophets might have their heads in the clouds and their hearts and their spirits in the eternal counsel of God; but their feet were on the ground with their fellow men and their ministry was in particular periods of history.

The book of Isaiah is in two major divisions, chapters 1—39 and chapters 40—66. Each of these divisions falls into smaller sections, to be noted as we read. Commentary and Bible dictionary should be consulted diligently throughout the study.

Isaiah 1—39

Matters Which Concern Judah and Jerusalem. (Chapters 1—12.) The first chapter of Isaiah forms a comprehensive introduction to Isaiah's prophesying. The chief function of a prophet is exemplified in denouncing sin and in declaring the certainty of judgment and the saving purpose of God.

Chapters 2—4 begin and end with oracles of blessing and glory, which come only through judgment and cleansing. Except for the beginning and the end, the section is a message of judgment. The righteous and the wicked receive the reward of their doings.

The parable of the vineyard (ch. 5) is of great beauty and power. "The vineyard of the LORD of hosts is the house of Israel . . . and he looked for justice but, behold oppression." (Vs. 7.) Note the woes proclaimed against oppressive greed, revelry, mockery, moral blindness, conceit of wisdom, and bribery. Announcement of fierce unnamed invaders closes the chapter.

Isaiah's vision and commission in the Temple (ch. 6) will repay endless study. The holiness and the glory of God are topics that challenge one's best thought. The prophet's task is a discouraging one, to deliver a message that will make hard hearts harder. We may remember the Gospel words, "This is the judgment, that the light is come into the world, and men loved the darkness rather than the light; for their works were evil." (John 3:19.)

Next, chapters 7:1—9:7 deal with Ahaz and his problems in connection with threats from Syria and Ephraim, which were attempting to force Judah into a coalition against Assyria. The prophet rebukes the faithlessness of the king and strives to reassure him, giving him the sign of the child Immanuel, God-with-us. Before this child, soon to be born, should reach years of discretion, the peril from Syria and Ephraim would be removed. Ahaz, against the protest of the prophet, called Assyria to his aid. Syria and Ephraim were overwhelmed, and Judah became vassal to Assyria. (II Kings 16 and 17.) Judah is threatened with invasion, desolation, and want. The people are exhorted to fear the Lord and find refuge in him. (Isa. 8:13-14.) Judgment prepares the way for mercy. (9:1-7.) The yoke will be broken, the war gear burned, and the Prince of Peace will reign in righteousness forever.

Note the judgments against the kingdom of Israel and the reasons for them. (9:8—10:4.) The Lord's anger is not appeased by punishment (9:12ff.), but only by repentance.

Study 10:5-34 for Isaiah's philosophy of history.

Chapter 11:1-10 pictures the ideal king, his endowment, and the idyllic conditions to prevail under his government. Note the universal extent of his kingdom in verses 9 and 10. In the remainder of chapter 11 the prophet promises for Ephraim and Judah restoration to their land and mutual reconcilation. The commentary and Bible dictionary will be especially useful in these parts.

Chapter 12 is made up of two beautiful hymns of thanksgiving and praise to God.

Concerning Foreign Nations. (Chapters 13—27.) The study of these chapters is interesting both religiously and historically. The commentary will clear up many obscurities of allusion and language.

The oracle against Babylon and its king stands high in prophetic literature. Note especially the triumph song over the king of Babylon. (14:4-20.) Destruction of Assyria is assured. (14:24-27.) Philistia is warned of false hopes of deliverance from oppression. (14:28-32.)

Chapters 15 and 16 pronounce judgment upon Moab. The gloom of the judgment is unrelieved except for the suggestion (16:2-5) that refuge may be found in Judah.

In chapter 17 judgment is pronounced against Syria and Ephraim (Israel). There will be restoration for a remnant after chastening and repentance (Vss. 6-8.) The invading Assyrians are denounced in verses 12-14.

Chapter 18 is an obscure encouragement to the Ethiopians who were alarmed over the aggressions of Assyria.

Chapter 19 is concerned with judgment upon Egypt, which is to be followed by some measure of reconciliation. (Vss. 18-22.) For a broader suggestion of peace between man and God note verses 23-25.

Chapter 20 warns Palestinian peoples against looking for help in alliances with Egypt and Ethiopia.

The vision of the fall of Babylon, chapter 21, seems to refer to a time when Babylon was not the oppressing power, but was hostile to Assyria, the oppressor. The chapter concludes with oracles upon Edom (symbolically called Dumah, "silence") and Arabia.

Chapter 22:1-14 presents a stinging rebuke to the frivolous people of Jerusalem, who in a time of despair turn to revelry and say, "Let us eat and drink, for to-morrow we shall die." This is followed by a denunciation of Shebna, the treasurer, who is to be superseded by Eliakim. It seems that the latter did not do well very long.

In chapter 23 judgment falls upon Tyre, with promise, it seems, of a kind of limited restoration "after the end of seventy years."

Chapters 24—27 present a vision of general world judgment, with particular foes of Israel in view. Israel also is disciplined. (27:9.) Songs of praise and devotion are mingled with the judgment, and the end of the vision is salvation.

Historical Situation in Reign of Hezekiah. (Chapters 28—33.) Many in Jerusalem advocated revolt from Assyria. They expected effective help from Egypt. Isaiah urged reliance upon the Holy One of Israel.

The opening verses of chapter 28 speak of Samaria. But at once (vs. 7) the word is to the men of Jerusalem. They, too, are guilty and are inviting judgment. The closing verses (23-29) by a beautiful parable teach that the Lord's judgments are measured and designed for discipline and improvement rather than for destruction.

Chapter 29. Affliction is destined for Ariel, God's "altar-hearth" (Jerusalem), and destruction for those that distress her. By discipline the chastened ones shall come to hear the truth and see the light (vs. 18), and shall "sanctify the Holy One of Jacob" (29:23).

Chapters 30 and 31 are much occupied with the prophet's remonstrance against seeking help from Egypt and his exhortations to his people to turn to the Lord. With God is deliverance, and he will destroy the Assyrian.

Chapter 32 portrays the ideal future with a righteous king. (32:1-8.) This and all such passages are of definite Messianic import. This ideal was always present and uppermost in the hearts of the prophets, growing in spirituality until Jesus came to rule the souls of men and to save his people from their sins.

Chapter 33. The despoiler is to be despoiled and the righteous oppressed delivered. Much of the chapter consists of psalms of praise. Note the exalted style and sentiment.

A Study in Contrasts and in History. (Chapters 34—39.) The first part of this section, chapters 34 and 35, is a study in contrasts. Chapter 34 gives a most graphic picture of judgment upon the nations and upon Edom in particular. Chapter 35 portrays as vividly the beauty and fertility of the land of the blessed.

Chapters 36—39, taken from II Kings 18:13—20:19, are included in the book of Isaiah for their importance in the history of Isaiah and Hezekiah. They differ from Kings in omitting the account of Hezekiah's submission (II Kings 18:14-16), in inserting Hezekiah's song of thanksgiving for recovery (38:9-20), and in some minor details. For discussion of the chronological problem consult the commentary.

Isaiah 40—66

The second major division of the book of Isaiah, chapters 40—66, is very different from the first. Subject matter and point of view are different. The student may investigate questions of authorship and date with the aid of commentary and Bible dictionary.

Nowhere else in the Bible will study be more amply rewarded. One feels helpless to suggest the majesty, beauty, and power of the prophet's teaching. His own words speak best for themselves. But of course all available study helps should be used. Many obscurities will need to be cleared up. Knowledge of the relevant history is indispensable. Modern translations will be found very helpful.

Eventual Return from Exile. (Chapters 40—48.) These chapters emphasize especially the eventual return from exile in Babylon, the greatness and the saving purpose of God, and the place of Cyrus in the accomplishment of God's plan.

In the prologue (40:1-11) the student will find one of the most magnificent treasures of inspired poetry, music, and spiritual insight in the Bible. Let each one study it until it sings itself anew in his soul. The rest of the chapter teaches the infinity of God, the folly of idolatry, and God's loving care for his people.

In chapter 41 Cyrus appears, a mighty conqueror, a terror to the nations. But Israel has nothing to fear. The Lord, Israel's Redeemer, has raised up Cyrus for his own gracious purposes.

The Servant of Jehovah is introduced in 42:1-4. The Servant is Israel, actual or ideal. The idealization progresses until the Servant becomes the individual incarnation of divine redeeming love and sacrifice. See the passages 49:1-6; 50:4-9; 52:13—53:12. The only realization of the ideal Servant was in the person, the ministry, the sacrifice, and the victory of Jesus Christ. The next verses (42:5—43:7) follow upon the announcement of the ideal Servant with rebuke for the blindness of the actual servant and assurance of the unchangeable saving purpose of God.

Israel is summoned to witness from experience to the revealing and saving work of God. (43:8-13.) There will be a new exodus, this time from Babylon. (Vss. 14-21.) Deliverance is wrought, not for Israel's merit but because Jehovah blots out his people's transgressions for his own sake. (Vss. 22-28.) Strangers see the blessedness of Israel and are induced to join themselves to him. (44:1-5.)

Israel is again summoned to witness to Jehovah's sole deity on the ground that he alone declares and sets in order future events. Idolatry is folly. Israel is charged to remember these things. (44:6-23.)

The work of Cyrus is portrayed (44:24—45:25), with its effect upon the spread of the knowledge of God. It all has its place in God's revealing purpose. "Look unto me, and be ye saved, all the ends of the earth: for I am God, and there is none else." (45:22.)

In chapter 46 the idol gods of Babylon take to flight, "a burden to the weary beast." In contrast, the Lord carries and delivers his people.

Chapter 47 is a song of triumph over Babylon, which had been God's instrument of discipline for Israel but had shown no mercy.

Chapter 48 repeats briefly arguments contained in previous chapters, with reproaches for the dullness and sin of the people. It closes with a call to the exiles to go forth from Babylon and say, "The Lord hath redeemed his servant Jacob."

Servant of Jehovah and Redemption. (Chapters 49—55.) This section emphasizes the mission of the Servant of Jehovah and the glory of redeemed Zion. The Servant passages usually listed have been noted in connection with chapter 42, but they by no means cover all the material that bears upon the Servant. The ideal Servant is present to the prophet's thought in all his teaching.

In 49:1-6 the Servant, addressing the nation, expresses regret that his mission has not been successful. But he is assured that God is his strength and that his mission far exceeds its previously expressed or recognized purpose. "It is too light a thing that thou shouldest be my servant to raise up the tribes of Jacob . . . I will also give thee for a light to the Gentiles, that thou mayest be my salvation unto the end of the earth." (49:6.) In 50:4-9 the Servant discloses his complete self-surrender to God, and his confidence, with the help of God, in the final victory of his righteous cause. The final passage of the series, 52:13—53:12, is an account of the Servant's sufferings and death, to be followed by future glory. We must, for the most part, omit details of interpretation here. But we may note that to the prophet's mind the Servant seems to be an Eternal Person, and that the only historical or imaginable realization of the prophet's thought is in the Jesus Christ of the Gospels.

The passages in this section relating to Zion redeemed include 49:14-26, 51:17—52:6, and chapter 54. Zion is figured as a woman, now desolate, bereaved, and afflicted; but soon to be reunited to her divine husband, to have her children restored, and to be herself clothed in garments of beauty and rejoicing. Also the people of Israel are urged to put away their fears and put their confidence in God, and to make ready for the salvation to come. (50:1-3; 51:1-16; ch. 55.) The student may profitably compare the content of this whole section (chs. 49—55) with the program outlined in 40:1-11.

Blessedness and Doom. (Chapters 56—66.) This final section describes the glory and blessedness of the true people of God and the doom of the unbelieving.

Chapter 56:1-8 shows that physical or racial considerations do not exclude from the privileges of the people of God. This is followed by a denunciation of evil rulers, worthless shepherds that devour the flock. (56:9—57:2.) The rest of chapter 57 condemns idolatrous and superstitious practices and promises forgiveness to the contrite.

Chapter 58 sets forth the conditions of right relations with God, the acceptable fast, right neighborly behavior, the keeping of the Sabbath, and the accompanying blessings.

Chapter 59 is a general confession of sin, with threat of divine judgment and promise of gracious visitation to those that turn from transgression.

Chapters 60—62 belong together. They are full of the blessedness and glory of Zion redeemed. Wealth, splendor, return of exiles, subservience of strangers and kings, and righteousness are mentioned as items of the blessedness and glory. The Christian will realize that the description of material blessedness must be minimized, remembering that the prophets often meant to express high spiritual realities under seemingly very material figures.

Chapter 63:1-6 is an oracle of judgment against Jehovah's foes. After a vivid description of the loving-kindness of the Lord (63:7-9), there follows a confession of Israel's sin and a penitential prayer (63:10—64:12). The study of this passage will furnish valuable spiritual exercise.

The last two chapters of the book announce rewards for the faithful and punishments for the faithless. Idolatry and supersition are denounced, and a golden age is promised to the servants of the Lord. Study 66:1-2 for a lesson of high spiritual value.

JEREMIAH

Many do not hesitate to call Jeremiah the greatest of the prophets, his only rival for the title being Isaiah. Probably more would call him the most interesting. Some have a tendency to place their preference upon the one that they have studied last. At any rate, Jeremiah is the best known of all the prophets. He reveals many details of his personal life and of his emotional and spiritual experiences. So we come to know him as a great soul, a most admirable and lovable character.

Jeremiah lived and ministered through the approach and the completion of Jerusalem's tragedy. Men and circumstances furnished him small comfort or solace. God was his only refuge. Temple, ark, and sacrifices were passing away, and Jeremiah was privileged to see that these things were secondary—that the prime essential in true godliness was the law written upon the heart. He was the first definitely to make religion independent of external helps and to emphasize its purely spiritual basis.

The serious student will find that one of the most valuable results of his study of the book of Jeremiah will be in his coming to know the prophet himself. He will find that he was no mere weeping prophet. He could weep, but it was from tender love for his erring and perishing people. He was one of the bravest, truest, and tenderest of all Bible characters. In his experiences and emotions he is often compared with Jesus Christ. For great spiritual profit study him in his book.

The chronological arrangement in this book is irregular. For light upon chronology, historical connection, and general questions of interpretation the student will of course constantly consult the commentary, the Bible dictionary, and any other available helps.

The book of Jeremiah does not fall naturally into distinct sections, consecutively arranged. The best division seems to be chapter by chapter, yet certain groupings of chapters may be noted as we read.

Jeremiah, a young man of sensitive and retiring disposition, is called to a task as heroic as any prophet ever faced. He is enjoined to speak the Lord's word without fear, and is assured of the Lord's presence and support. (Ch. 1.)

Judgment but Not Complete Destruction. (Chapters 2—33.) The first four chapters of this section, chapters 2—6, are sometimes grouped together as picturing religious conditions in Judah before Josiah's reform. This is convenient and generally plausible, though 3:10 may indicate that Josiah's efforts have already been put into operation. From these chapters the student may learn much about the teaching and the methods of the prophets in general and of Jeremiah in particular. They stress Israel's obligation to God for land and national life (2:6-7), and the futility of idolatry (2:28). Jeremiah pleads with Israel to repent, with promise of healing for the penitent and the spiritual worshipers. (Ch. 3.) Chapter 4 contains impassioned pleas for amendment, along with anguished apprehension of inevitable judgment. The prophet paints a weird picture of chaos returned. (4:23-26.) Chapters 5 and 6 are much alike in condemning the sin of

Jerusalem, in threatening judgment by a mighty nation from afar, and in rebuking the people for spurning the words of the prophets. All classes of the people, including prophets and priests, were guilty. But of course these were true prophets to whom the people should have given heed. Note the recurring idea, "I will not make a full end," denoting the disciplinary purpose of the judgment. Also note (6:14), "Peace, peace; when there is no peace." "Peace" means "right relations" in the broadest sense.

Chapter 7 is one of the most significant in the book. "Amend your ways and your doings." (Vs. 3.) Morality rather than ritual is the basic requirement of God's law. The place of heathen sacrifice shall become a place for burial. (Vs. 32; see marginal translation and commentaries.)

Chapter 8 gives further delineations of guilt, folly, and judgment. The birds of the air know and follow their mysterious ways; "but my people know not the judgment of the LORD." (Vs. 7.) Tragedy comes on apace. The prophet longs for comfort against sorrow.

Chapter 9. The prophet laments the prevalence of deceit. "Shall I not visit them for these things? saith the LORD." (Vs. 9.) Perhaps the portrayals of punishment increase in horror. For a gem upon the true glory of man see verses 23 and 24.

Chapter 10:1-16 describes the vanity of idols, and contrasts the living Creator God. Punishment for transgression must come. Discipline must be accepted, with the plea that it be in measure and not unto utter destruction. (Vs. 24.)

Chapters 11 and 12 form one prophecy. The people have been unfaithful to the covenant, probably the Book of the Law found in the Temple in the eighteenth year of Josiah. Punishment is sure. This has been thought to represent Jeremiah's attitude to Josiah's reformation. (11:1-17.) The hostility of the men of Anathoth to the prophet is abruptly introduced, and sentence against them pronounced. (11: 18-23.) The prophet is perplexed at the prosperity of the wicked. He must meet further perplexities, and play the man. It is a time of judgment when "no flesh shall have peace." The evil neighbors shall be judged, but may be restored if they learn righteous ways. (Ch. 12.)

Chapter 13 has an impressive symbol of a linen girdle, spoiled when out of place and exposed to destructive agencies. So is Israel when astray from the Lord. Four woes of punishment follow.

In chapters 14 and 15 the prophet makes a severe drought (14:1-6) the starting point for a long dialogue with the Lord. He acknowledges the people's sin and pleads for pardon in vain. (14:7-12.) False prophets receive their sentence. (14:13-16.) The dialogue and pleading continue in the same tenor until the latter part of chapter 15, where the prophet laments his own hard task and hard fate, and receives reassurance from the Lord.

Chapter 16. Jeremiah is to live a life apart, without family or other normal human associations, because of the woes that sweep over the land and people. These woes are to be followed by great deliverance.

Chapter 17. Heathen worship is condemned. (17:1-4.) After other oracles the prophet defends his ministry. (17:12-18.) Sabbath-keeping is made the test of a rising or falling people.

The potter's clay (ch. 18) illustrates God's ways with men. The application is not favorable to the men of Judah. They plot against the prophet who, in Old Testament style, invokes justice upon them.

The overthrow of Jerusalem, with graphic details, is illustrated by the shattering of a potter's vessel that cannot be made whole again. (Ch. 19.)

Chapter 20. Pashur, a dignitary in the Temple, puts Jeremiah in stocks because of the preceding prophecies. He is denounced and sentenced to the penalties of exile. Jeremiah then complains bitterly of the lot of an unwelcome prophet, from which he cannot escape.

Jeremiah (ch. 21) declares to Zedekiah that it is hopeless to resist Babylon, and counsels submission and surrender.

Chapter 22. Jeremiah is sent to the king's house and enjoins him to do justice. But disobedience brings judgment. (Vss. 1-9.) The rest of the chapter is mostly oracles against kings.

Chapter 23. Woe to evil and greedy shepherds! (Vss. 1-4.) One of the chief Messianic passages in Jeremiah is in verses 5-8. The rest of the chapter is a scathing denunciation of false prophets.

Chapter 24. The choice and the hope of the nation went as exiles with Jehoiachin in 597 b.c. The restoration will be of these choice spirits.

Chapter 25. The prophet's pleading has been in vain. Captivity is determined for seventy years, after which Babylon will be punished and all nations will drink the cup of God's fury.

Chapter 26. Jeremiah experiences the peril of speaking the truth, for which many have died. This is a very interesting study in biography and religious history.

Chapter 27. Two oracles upon submission to Nebuchadnezzar. As usual, Jeremiah is in opposition to the false prophets.

Chapter 28. Hananiah, a pugnacious false prophet, comes into conflict with Jeremiah, who stands firm, predicts Hananiah's early death, and is vindicated.

Chapter 29. Jeremiah sends a letter of sane counsel to the exiles in Babylon, who also are afflicted by false prophets. After a striking prophecy of the return from exile after seventy years (vss. 10-14), the fate of the false prophets is foretold.

Chapters 30 and 31 are often called by some such title as the Book of Comfort. Their theme is found in such lines as "Ye shall be my people, and I will be your God." (30:22.) The high point is the new convenant (31:31-34) in which religion becomes entirely spiritual and personal, a matter of personal reconciliation and fellowship with God.

Chapters 32—43 are mainly historical, and deal with events during the last two years leading up to and including the destruction of Jerusalem. Jeremiah suffers persecution, false accusation, harsh imprisonment, and cruel want. Through it all he stands bravely by the unpopular truth that Jerusalem is doomed, and that such is God's purpose in the interest of righteousness and true religion.

Chapter 32. At God's direction Jeremiah buys a field in Anathoth, when it is practically in the hands of the Chaldeans. He is perplexed, but is assured that there will be a restoration and normal tenure of land in the country.

Chapter 33 is full of promise of blessing after judgment. One of Jeremiah's distinctly Messianic passages is found in verses 14-18.

Infliction of Judgment Described. (Chapters 34—44.) In chapter 34, Jeremiah predicts that Jerusalem shall be taken and burned, and Zedekiah taken captive to Babylon. (Vss. 1-7.) The freeing and retaking of the Hebrew slaves apparently came about in connection with the history recorded in 37:5-10. The slaves were freed when fear of the Chaldeans ran high, and seized again when the besiegers withdrew. The thought was of a bribe to God, to be taken back when it seemed no longer necessary.

Chapters 35 and 36 go back to the reign of Jehoiakim. The Rechabites furnish a notable example of loyal obedience to their ancestor, in contrast with Judah's disobedience to the Lord. Hoping against hope that Judah may repent, Jeremiah prepares a book of prophecies, which produces some fear and probably more hostility in the court. Jehoiakim the king treats the book with insolent contempt.

Chapters 37 and 38 deal with the period of the siege of Jerusalem. Note the weakness of King Zedekiah, his secret consultations with Jeremiah, Jeremiah's sane counsel, the false accusations against the prophet, and his sufferings.

Chapter 39. Jerusalem is taken. Zedekiah, having disregarded the warnings of Jeremiah, suffers a sad fate. (Vss. 4-7.) Nebuchadnezzar looks to the welfare of Jeremiah. The prophet receives from the Lord a word of promise for Ebed-melech, the Ethiopian who had befriended him during his imprisonment.

Chapters 40—43. Nebuchadnezzar appointed Gedaliah governor of the remnant in Judah. Jeremiah chooses to remain in the land. (40: 2-6.) Gedaliah was moderate and practical, and the beginning of his administration promised well. But he was murdered and anarchy broke out. After some fighting to avenge his death, the victorious faction under Johanan gathered as many as possible of the remnant of Judah and went to Egypt for fear of the Chaldeans. The flight into Egypt was against the earnest protest of Jeremiah, who was taken along. For the characters involved in this history, consult the commentary and the Bible dictionary.

Jeremiah in Egypt protested (ch. 44) against the idolatry of his people. His protest was futile; and tradition has it that his enraged compatriots murdered him and buried him in the sand. This is the last that we know or hear of Jeremiah.

"Seekest thou great things for thyself? seek them not," is the great lesson of chapter 45, which records an appendix to Baruch's roll of chapter 36.

Prophecies Concerning the Nations. (Chapters 46—51.) These chapters may be passed over with a brief summation. The prophecies recorded here are of earlier date than the history we have just left. The nations against which judgment is pronounced are, in the order of mention in the book of Jeremiah, Egypt, Philistia, Moab, Ammon, Edom, Damascus, Kedar, Hazor, and Elam. These nations have been hostile to Israel and to Israel's God. In connection with the prophecy against Babylon there is promise of deliverance for Israel. (50:4ff.; 50:17ff.) God is exalted. (51:15ff.) There is a note of hope after judgment for Egypt, Moab, Ammon, and Elam. The sweep of the judgments thrusts home the truth that the earth is the Lord's, and that he is working to "bring in everlasting righteousness." (Dan. 9:24.)

Chapter 52 is a historical appendix of much the same substance as chapter 39. Both are taken from II Kings 24:18—25:30. One item in Jeremiah is not mentioned elsewhere, the deportation "in the three and twentieth year" of Nebuchadnezzar. (Vs. 30.)

THE LAMENTATIONS OF JEREMIAH

This little book, if it is rescued from neglect and receives the attention it deserves, will be found to be of great value and absorbing interest. It is to be studied as a unit, though it consists of five separate elegies portraying the sufferings and grief of the Jewish people in connection with the destruction of Jerusalem by Nebuchadnezzar in 586 B.C.

There is far more in these poems than mere fruitless repining and self-pity. These, indeed, are conspicuously absent. While the victims of the tragedy suffer keenly, their sufferings are so borne as to be, in Christian phrase, a means of grace. Mention of a few of the more obvious features of interest and value will now be made.

The book of Lamentations is of great historical and literary interest. Details of the siege and sack of Jerusalem are vividly presented. The reader feels that he is receiving the account from one who saw the calamity and was himself in the midst of it suffering most cruelly.

The poetic quality of the composition is very high. The pathos of sheer tragedy has seldom found more moving expression than, for example, in 4:9-11. Sensitive souls always respond to heroic souls in agony; and the literature that portrays such souls will always live, and will always be sought for the sense of fellowship in the world's woe that it furnishes to kindred souls. Lamentations is read by pious Israelites every Friday at the Jews' wailing place in Jerusalem, and in synagogues throughout the world on the anniversary of the burning of the Temple.

Religious teaching, always properly the chief quest in Bible study, is in the forefront of the thought throughout. There is no self-righteousness suggested, whether of the individual or of the nation. "The Lord is righteous." (1:18.) He has fulfilled his word of judgment, and his ways are justified to men. As for the people, they, with their prophets and their priests, have sinned, and their punishment is humbly and prayerfully accepted. Good examples, both in word and in spirit, are found for those who would confess their sin. The confession of sin and the humble acceptance of punishment as righteous are accompanied by fervent prayer and hope for forgiveness and restoration to God's favor. Here also is a good example for religious people of all nations and of all ages. A surpassingly beautiful expression of faith and hope is found in 3:22-41.

A note of imprecation against foes, not quite rare in the Psalms and other Old Testament Scriptures, is found in 1:22 and 3:64-66. Such utterances, though they may be directed against those who are really God's enemies, seem out of keeping with the ideal of the gospel in the New Testament.

EZEKIEL

Ezekiel, a young Jewish priest, was taken captive to Babylon with Jehoiachin in 597 B.C. His prophetic ministry began five years later, in the fifth year of King Jehoiachin's captivity, and by his own dating continued for twenty-two years, his latest mentioned date being the twenty-seventh year. (29:17.) Therefore the period of his activity covered the last tragic years of Jerusalem before the exile, the destruction of the city and the Temple, and about sixteen years of the exile itself. Being already a captive the prophet did not pass through the sufferings of the final siege and burning of the city himself; but he realized them so keenly that he makes the scenes of sin, judgment, and desolation all but live and move before the eyes of the reader.

The book of Ezekiel is the finished work of the prophet himself, and is well arranged chronologically and topically. The observant reader will have noted that such is not the case with Isaiah and Jeremiah.

Ezekiel is, not merely by traditional terminology but in the absolute sense, a great prophet—one of the supremely great. His imagination is marvelous in sweep and in sustained flight. He has been described as the greatest literary artist of the ancient world. But more than that, he is an inspired architect of the Kingdom of God. Through all the tragedy of Jerusalem, which he recognized as just and necessary for the glory of the holy God, he saw as the final goal a redeemed, righteous, and blessed City of God, with a new name, Jehovah-shammah, which is being interpreted, "The Lord is there." The visions of Ezekiel begin and end in glory: at the beginning the vision of the glory of the Lord, at the end the glory of the City of God.

The reader of Ezekiel greatly needs to cultivate and use the imagination—to sit where he sat (3:15) in earnest meditation, to see what he saw, and to feel what he felt. By such means the word of the Lord through the prophet may most effectively reach us.

The book falls into three major divisions. Chapters 1—24 deal with the sin, the judgment, and the inevitable destruction of Jerusalem. Chapters 25—32 deal with judgment upon neighboring heathen peoples. Chapters 33—48 deal with the restoration of the people, now chastened and cleansed from idolatry, to the land; the reunion of all Israel, the new covenant, the new Temple, the new distribution of land, and the new city.

For matters of detailed explanation the student will consult the commentary throughout the study of the book. These notes can attempt no more than to indicate some of the points of high interest and importance, with a minimum of comment.

Sin; Judgment; Destruction of Jerusalem. (Chapters 1—24.) It is fitting that Ezekiel, whose book is devoted to the vindication of the holiness, justice, and sovereignty of God, should begin with a vision of his glory. (Ch. 1.) The prophet saw a whirling storm cloud in the north, with glowing colors and lightnings playing incessantly. His prophetic discernment was quickened, and he saw in the storm a vision of cherubim above which appeared the firmament and the throne of Jehovah. The magnificence of the spectacle and the mystery of its organization and movement appropriately suggest the glory and the mystery of God's being and of his ways. But note the prophet's reverent reserve. He carefully refrains from even suggesting that he saw God in his vision. For example, "This was the appearance of the likeness of the glory of the LORD." (1:28.) For detailed comment see the commentary; for the cherubim, see the Bible dictionary.

Chapters 2 and 3 give the account of the prophet's commission, in immediate connection with the preceding vision. This commission is regarded by some as threefold, by others as one commission in three steps. In any case it will hold and reward the attention of the student. Note the eating of the roll, symbolizing inspiration; the appointment as watchman; and the command to speak God's words courageously to a people who would not hear. This last was usually the task of a true prophet. The captives to whom Ezekiel prophesied were still rebellious. And they probably believed that deliverance was immediately at hand, before due and full discipline had been inflicted.

In chapters 4 and 5 the prophet was commanded to perform certain actions symbolizing siege, famine, pestilence, death by the sword, fire, and exile, all the woes that came upon Jerusalem in the execution of God's judgment. Because of the strangeness of some of these actions, it has been supposed that they were not really performed, but only presented ideally. However, from what we know of the ways of the prophets in presenting and emphasizing their messages, we may rather believe that they were actually done. Such actions made deep impressions upon the ancient Israelites and kindred peoples.

Chapter 6 pronounces judgment against the mountains of Israel.

The idol shrines with their unclean heathen festivals were usually found in the mountains. Destruction must fall upon altars and worshipers. But a remnant shall escape, of whom it is said, "And they shall know that I am the LORD." (6:10.) The reader should note these words well. It is Ezekiel's favorite expression. He uses it or its close equivalent about fifty times to emphasize God's gracious revealing purpose in judgment as well as in redemption.

Chapter 7 is an oracle of overwhelming destruction. "An end, the end is come upon the four corners of the land." (7:2.) Though some of the people escape, their escape brings no brightness. The only ray of light in the chapter appears at the end in the prophet's formula, "They shall know that I am the LORD." This indicates the gracious purpose of the direst judgment, and marks the first step toward repentance and reconciliation.

Chapters 8—11 describe various idolatries and abominations practiced by the people of Jerusalem. The punishments which must ensue are presented in vivid figure, and culminate in the departure of the glory of the Lord from the city. The prophet is, of course, seeing in vision things that are invisible to the physical eye; but he is nevertheless portraying realities, and his vision of judgment was literally fulfilled in the destruction of the city and the Temple.

The reader may note in connection with his study of this section that the glory of the Lord, according to the vision which he saw in the plain, was never far from the prophet's thought. He mentions it or alludes to it several times, and it was probably always present to him as he received and delivered the revelation of God's works and ways.

We may note a few further thoughts in these important chapters. The cherubim with the wheels beside them, forming the chariot that bears the glory of the Lord, face in all four directions. "They turned not as they went" (10:11); "they went every one straight forward" (10:22). There is no occasion for turning. The prophet teaches graphically that the Lord's purposes cannot change, but must go straight forward to completion.

"The men that devise mischief, and give wicked counsel in the city" (11:2) find their confidence vain. They thought that the present and approaching woes would soon be past. The prophet was directed to denounce their sin and to proclaim their fall by the sword. As this word was uttered one of the leaders of evil counsel died. Ezekiel cried out, "Ah Lord GOD! wilt thou make a full end of the remnant of Israel?" (11:13.) He received a reply that was heartening and gracious in final purpose. He was told that the exiles, himself and his fellows, were the real objects of God's favor. The inhabitants of Jerusalem have said to them, "Get you far from the LORD; unto us is this land given for a possession." (11:15.) But the Lord says, "Whereas I have scattered them among the countries, yet will I be to them a sanctuary for a little while in the countries where they are come." (11:16.) The Lord also declares that he will bring back the exiles and give them the land of Israel, and put a new spirit within them and give them a heart of flesh that they may keep his ordinances and be his people. But as for the rebellious sinners in Jerusalem, he will "bring their way upon their own heads." Compare Jeremiah 24 and 31:31-34.

As for the doomed city, the cherubim lifted their wings and the wheels beside them; and the glory of the Lord departed, to return no more until the establishment of the ideal New Jerusalem. So the vision was ended, and the prophet spoke to those in captivity all the things that the Lord had showed him.

The next section to be taken for study covers chapters 12—24, finishing the first major division of Ezekiel. With symbolic action and parable, with allegory and exhortation, the prophet stresses the gross and persistent wickedness of Jerusalem and the necessity of her destruction for the honor of God and for righteousness' sake. Throughout the section the imminence of the judgment is emphasized.

In chapter 12 the prophet performs acts symbolic of flight, exile, and famine. Here the prophet is a sign to rebellious Israel. "Like as I have done, so shall it be done unto them." (12:11.) There were many in Israel who could not believe that the threatened doom was at hand. They believed that the vision would fail or that it was for times very far off. Their unbelief received a stern rebuke. (Vss. 21-28.)

Chapter 13 gives impressive warning against false prophets who "prophesy out of their own heart . . . and have seen nothing." Such prophets declare that all is well when nothing is well. Their words are pleasant on the surface and for the moment, and they are greatly preferred by many undiscerning people. Much light will be shed upon some obscure matters in this chapter by the commentary.

Chapter 14 contains a stinging rebuke to inquirers who come to the prophet with their idols set up in their hearts and themselves given over to their iniquity. The prophet who answers such inquirers will in the very act be proved a false prophet, and prophet and inquirers will bear equal punishment. The commentary will be of help in the interpretation of verse 9.

The latter half of this chapter furnishes interesting light upon the justice of the Lord and upon some of the ways of his providential instruction. A few righteous men in a land will not avail to deliver a multitude of guilty sinners. But in Jerusalem some of the guilty will survive and be taken to join the exiles of earlier deportations, in order that the latter may see their ways and their doings and be comforted for the necessary destruction of Jerusalem.

Chapter 15 is a gem, a parable so transparent that explanation is scarcely needed. Yet the reader may find the commentary helpful.

Chapter 16 is an extended allegory picturing the history of Jerusalem and God's dealing with her from the beginning. On the side of Jerusalem it is a history of perpetual ingratitude, unfaithfulness, and rebellion. Every Bible reader has noted how often the prophets represent idolatry under the figure of unchastity. And this was no mere figure, for the prevailing idolatrous worship was accompanied by lascivious rites. The portrayal is carried out at length and in detail here. One should not overlook the fact that this fearful arraignment is followed by a word of grace: "I will remember my covenant." (Vs. 60.) God does not abandon his people. For any needed elucidation see the commentary.

Chapter 17. In allegory or parable the faithless and tragic career of King Zedekiah is described. The portrayal is skillfully and artistically done, and is one of the best examples of Ezekiel as a great literary artist. The chapter closes with a truly Messianic promise.

Chapter 18. It was not easy for the ancient Israelite to realize fully the principle of personal rather than corporate or national responsibility in matters of righteousness and guilt. Jeremiah and Ezekiel taught it emphatically. Today men still need to face the principle honestly. We are adept at finding scapegoats. But "the soul that sinneth, it shall die." (Vs. 4.)

Chapter 19 is a lamentation over the captivity of Jehoahaz in Egypt and of Jehoiachin in Babylon. The language is figurative, but of unmistakable meaning. "Thy mother" is the people Israel. The best suggestion for the true meaning of the first clause in verse 10 is, "Thy mother is like a vine in her height."

The concluding chapters, 20—24, of the first major division of Ezekiel may here be briefly summarized. In response to the inquiries of certain elders of Israel the prophet recites the abominations of their fathers, in which succeeding generations have persisted, and declares that the Lord will cause them to pass under the rod. (Ch. 20.) The avenging sword stands out in chapter 21. Obscurities in this chapter will drive the reader to the commentary. Chapter 22 carries on the sweeping arraignment. Prophets, priests, princes, and people of the land are all guilty and await destruction from the Lord. Chapter 23 pictures idolatrous Samaria and Jerusalem under the figure of two erring sisters. The reader will remember the figure, less developed, in Jeremiah 3:6-11. In chapter 24 the word of the Lord informs the prophet that the siege of Jerusalem is begun. The end is at hand. At the evening of the day the prophet's wife dies. He is commanded to show no outward sign of mourning. So Israel will be stunned by the tragedy of Jerusalem, and Ezekiel will be a "sign unto them."

Space requires that the remainder of Ezekiel be passed over rapidly. Fortunately the nature of the material is such that brief notice seems to be sufficient for the present purpose.

Judgment upon Neighboring Peoples. (Chapters 25—32.) The next major division of the book may be dismissed with a few lines. Judgments against neighboring peoples, chapters 25—32, are all of one piece. The peoples had been hostile, envious, and generally injurious toward Israel through the centuries. They were ready to gloat over Israel's calamities, and to take part in or to take advantage of the devastations. They, perhaps Tyre especially, had furnished perpetual incentives to idolatry. Egypt had been the evil and betraying genius of Israel in international relations. And their sins, regardless of their attitude to Israel, abundantly merited the utmost of judgment. Their punishment was a part of the progress of the Kingdom of God. For the prophet's own summary of the purpose of these judgments see 28:24-36.

Restoration of the People. (Chapters 33—48.) The third major division of Ezekiel falls naturally into two sections, chapters 33—39 and chapters 40—48. The first section, dealing with the restoration of Israel, offers some of the prophet's noblest chapters, but they are for the most part easy to understand, and consist partly of expansions and counterparts of matter that has gone before.

Chapter 33 repeats the prophet's commission as a watchman, and vindicates the fairness of Jehovah's ways (compare chapter 3). The prophet is informed by a messenger that Jerusalem is taken (compare 24:25-27 with 33:21-22), and he is assured that doubters shall know "that a prophet hath been among them."

Chapter 34 presents the contrast between good and evil shepherds, with an emphatic Messianic note in the picture of the good shepherd, the ideal David. Our thoughts turn to him who said so truly, "I am the good shepherd." (John 10:11.)

Chapter 35. Another sweeping sentence of destruction against Mount Seir (Edom). "And they shall know that I am the LORD."

Chapter 36. The restoration of the mountains of Israel. See chapter 6. Note that the Lord saves for his own honor. (Vss. 20ff.) Compare the new heart (vs. 26) with the same in 11:19.

Chapter 37 is perhaps the best-known chapter in Ezekiel. In figure the prophet sees a national resurrection. He symbolizes a reunion of all Israel. (Vss. 15-17.) He portrays the Messianic Kingdom, with a cleansed and restored people and an ideal shepherd and king. The vision is still in process of realization, for men continue to be blind, stubborn, and earthy.

Chapters 38 and 39 foretell God's final victory over his rebellious heathen foes. For detailed explanation see the commentary and the Bible dictionary.

The final section of the book, chapters 40—48, sets forth in minute detail the structure, furnishings, and ordinances of the ideal new Temple; also regulations for government and a plan for a new distribution of the land among the tribes. The elaborate regulation of the Temple service was to teach the people the difference between the holy and the profane. The regulations for government and land tenure emphasized advanced principles of justice. Ezekiel had a magnificent conception of the Kingdom of God. Perhaps Bible students seldom do him justice.

The account of the structure of the new Temple is not easy for us to understand in detail, and some of the terms used are obscure. Carefully prepared plans are found in the commentary. Notice a suggestion of Ezekiel's ideal of government in 45:8, "My princes shall no more oppress my people"; and in chapter 47 the vision of the healing waters flowing from the Temple and widening as they flow. Compare Revelation 22:1-2.

DANIEL

The book of Daniel furnishes some of the most thrilling Bible stories which have delighted and instructed children through the ages. But the vivid portrayal of inflexible moral courage and heroic religious faith gives gripping interest and power to the stories, not for children and youth alone, but for all.

Nowhere is a sensible commentary more needed than in the study of this book. Even with such help some puzzling problems may remain. But on the whole it may be said that it is not too great a task to understand Daniel reasonably well, and that the vital lessons are very clear. The student should use study helps diligently and try to get the meaning of the book in its entirety.

Daniel is short enough to be studied as a unit, and its parts are closely related. But it divides itself naturally into two equal sections.

The first section, chapters 1—6, describes experiences of the young Hebrew captives, Daniel and his three companions, at the court of Babylon. It is in this section particularly that great moral and religious lessons are driven home to the heart of the individual.

Daniel and His Companions. (Chapters 1—6.) In chapter 1 the young men are strangers at the court with prospect of attaining to positions of privilege by conforming to court standards. But the court standards are contrary to the law of God. A true conscience can give only one answer to the problem of the Hebrew youths. They must obey God's Law at whatever cost. They do obey, and their faithful obedience does not hinder their preferment. The plain living required by their Law rather promoted high thinking which fitted them for advancement at court. A poet has told us that often the path of duty is the way to glory. So in the case before us it proved to be. But we should recognize that Daniel and his friends were faithful from no calculating motive of earthly reward.

A few of the more prominent teachings of chapters 2—6 may be pointed out in a brief summary, with more detailed study left to the interest of the student. In chapter 2 we have the account of Nebuchadnezzar's dream of a great image. The king demanded of his wise men, as a test of their powers, that they tell him the dream, which he will not disclose (see 2:5, A.S.V. margin), as well as its interpretation. They could not divine the dream, and were therefore under sentence of death by the king's edict. God revealed the dream to Daniel, who was under the same sentence, in a vision, and Daniel gave to the king the interpretation. For the kingdoms symbolized in the dream image, see the commentary. The high point of the teaching in the chapter is presented in verse 44, which declares the eternal and universal reign of God. This eternal kingdom of God is truly the ruling theme, not only of the book of Daniel, but of the whole Scripture as well. Other teachings also are obvious, and will thrust themselves upon the attention of the student.

Chapters 3 and 6 may be grouped together as stories of conflict. Three young men, chapter 3, and one old man, chapter 6, are pitted against the proud and despotic world powers of their time. Their only offense is loyalty to their God and to the requirements of their religion. They were heroes of faith, ready to suffer martyrdom, and in prospect did so suffer. They were marvelously delivered from death, and their experiences illustrate our maxim that one with God is a majority. Note the recognition of the true God and the glory ascribed to him by the heathen rulers in the closing words of each chapter.

Chapters 4 and 5 show the folly of pride and sacrilege that leave God out of account. Nebuchadnezzar, chapter 4, is brought to extreme humiliation as a consequence of his insensate vainglory. Belshazzar, chapter 5, in the very act of desecrating the sacred vessels from the Temple in Jerusalem, receives sentence of the loss of his kingdom, and in the immediate execution of the sentence is slain. After his humiliation Nebuchadnezzar is restored, and gives praise and honor to the King of heaven who is able to humble those who walk in pride and whose dominion is an everlasting dominion. And Belshazzar bestows upon Daniel, the interpreter of God's judgment, what recognition and reward he can before his death "in that night."

In the chapters so far under consideration the character, the majesty, and the sovereignty of God are strongly emphasized. The Lord reigneth! And since, as will perhaps appear more clearly in the following section, the purpose of the book is to encourage and strengthen the pious Jews under the savage persecutions of Antiochus Epiphanes, we should not suppose that the former chapters have not some direct reference to the arrogance and sacrilege of this ruthless tyrant.

Visions of Daniel. (Chapters 7—12.) These chapters constitute the second section of our book. They relate visions of Daniel with their interpretation. For the study of these chapters the need for the commentary is as great and urgent as for the study of any other part of the Bible. And it must be used with diligence if one would hope to understand. The Bible dictionary also will be found highly useful.

The visions are, in the main, a series of presentations of history extending from the Babylonian Empire to the end of the career of Antiochus Epiphanes. Nations and powers that come into view are Babylon, Medo-Persia, Greece (Alexander and his successors), Syria, and Egypt.

Throughout the visions two consummations are in view. The consummation of earthly power, hostile to God and to his people, is in Antiochus Epiphanes, figured by the little horn of chapters 7 and 8, the prince that shall come (9:26), and the vile person (11:21). Anti-

ochus became symbolical of all that is godless and lawless; he furnishes much to Paul's conception of the man of sin in II Thessa-
lonians 2. The other consummation which follows is in the reign of
God or the kingdom of the saints of the Most High. See 7:18, 27 and
9:24. The latter passage brings out the two ideas clearly: "To finish
transgression, and to make an end of sins, and to make reconciliation
for iniquity, and to bring in everlasting righteousness." The world is
still waiting for this consummation. The visions in chapter 7 and 8
are interpreted in the one case by an unnamed interpreter, in the
other by the angel Gabriel. Any further needed help may be found
in the commentary.

In chapter 9 special notice should be taken of Daniel's prayer of
confession and supplication. This prayer offers much of valuable and
helpful suggestion for the penitent sinner's approach to God. It
needs only the further revelation that brought fuller light in the
New Testament gospel.

Particular diligence will be needed in two especially difficult passages, 9:20-27 and chapter 11. These are mentioned in this way, not
that detailed explanation may be offered here, but that the necessity
of the commentary may receive final emphasis. When all is done
9:20-27 may still leave unsolved problems. Chapter 11, introduced
by chapter 10, sketches the history of the peoples with whom the
Jews have relations from Cyrus the Persian to the death of Antiochus
Epiphanes. Events in the history of the Greek kingdoms of Syria
and Egypt (the North and the South) are given in detail. Their
wars with each other receive particular attention. These wars, with
their accompanying outrages and treacheries, lead up to the rise of
Antiochus, whose career and fall are fully described. All of this
chapter is so obscure that it will scarcely be understood at all except
through the study of the history as it is given in plain language in
the commentary. But the student who works out and understands
this section will have gone far toward understanding the visions of
Daniel or, we may even say, will have attained that goal.

Chapter 12, with further allusions to the distress of the persecution,
gives assurance of the final blessedness of the wise and of the end of
evils.

THE MINOR PROPHETS

HOSEA through MALACHI

PATRICK H. CARMICHAEL

THE MINOR PROPHETS

Hosea—The Prophet of Love

Joel—The Prophet of Hope

Amos—The Prophet of Justice

Obadiah—The Prophet of Judgment upon Edom

Jonah—The Prophet of Outreach

Micah—The Prophet of Justice and Love

Nahum—The Prophet of Judgment Against Assyria

Habakkuk—The Philosopher

Zephaniah—The Prophet of Universal Judgment

Haggai—The Prophet of Reconstruction

Zechariah—The Prophet of Reconstruction and Re-establishment

Malachi—The Prophet of Judgment and Mercy

THE MINOR PROPHETS

Outline

I. Description of an Unhappy Home Life. Chapters 1—3
- A. Prophet directed to marry Gomer. 1:2
- B. The birth of three children. 1:3-9
- C. A message of hope. 1:10—2:1
- D. Denunciation of sin. 2:2-7
- E. Degeneracy and misery. 2:8-13
- F. Pardon assured if repentant. 2:14—3:5

II. A Message to Israel. Chapters 4—14
- A. Sin and need for repentance. 4:1—6:3
  - 1. Religious leaders lead in sin. 4:1—5:15
  - 2. A call to repentance, with promise. 6:1-3
- B. Punishment surely follows sin. 6:4—10:15
  - 1. Halfhearted repentance not enough. 6:4-11
  - 2. Sin is followed by judgment. 7:1—8:14
  - 3. Israel's unfaithfulness. 9:1—10:15
- C. God's love for Israel. 11:1—13:16
  - 1. A father's love for a child. 11:1-11
  - 2. Independence must give place to dependence. 11:12—12:6
  - 3. A God of mercy and of judgment. 12:7—13:16
- D. An appeal for repentance, with promise. 14:1-9

Comments

This, the first of the so-called minor prophecies, was probably written a few years later than Amos, as the reader will discover from a study of the commentary and the Bible dictionary. It is incoherently written, in poor style, giving a brief account of a long service. Its message is given in two major divisions, as indicated by the outline above. One is a terrifying description of an unhappy home life, the other a message to Israel condemning her for sin, pronouncing the judgment of God upon her, and pleading with her to repent.

The first three chapters are unique in many ways. God is represented as directing his prophet to marry a woman of the street. The anticipated disappointments and heartaches of subsequent years are described with vividness. The separation, and the prophet's ultimately buying her back as an expression of unfailing love, are impressively recounted here. It is not surprising that there have been many conflicting opinions expressed with reference to the true interpretation of this section of the prophecy. For a full discussion see the Bible dictionary and the commentary. Whether this be an account of the experience of Hosea or merely an allegory, what the prophet wanted to say to his contemporaries and to succeeding generations is clear. He was representing symbolically the relationship which God sustained to his people and his intense desire for their redemption. In a sense we have here an Old Testament version of the New Testament story of the prodigal son.

The second section of the book contains a somewhat detailed story of the relationship which Israel sustained to her God. The reader will be impressed with the oft-repeated statement characterizing Israel as an adulterous nation. When this term is used to describe the relationship of Israel to her God, it means spiritual unfaithfulness, but as the idol worship was characterized by gross immorality, the metaphor is singularly appropriate.

Here Hosea denounced the people of Israel for their sin and affirmed their need for repentance, declaring that the religious leaders have led the people into sin. This may not always have been deliberate on their part, nevertheless it had been true. In the sixth chapter the prophet calls upon his people to repent as the only way whereby they may be assured of God's blessing.

Over against the promise of blessings there is the assurance that punishment follows sin, thus placing before them the alternative. Realizing the tendency of human nature to respond emotionally in times of impending danger the prophet reminds them that mere emotional repentance is not enough. He sounds a warning against a certain type of revivalism the results of which are no more enduring than "a morning cloud, and as the dew that goeth early away." (6:4.) Of those whose repentance is no more lasting he says, "I hewed them by the prophets; I have slain them by the words of my mouth . . ." (6:5.) Then follows what may be regarded as the key verse of the prophecy: "For I desire goodness, and not sacrifice; and the knowledge of God more than burnt-offerings." (6:6.)

Chapters 9 and 10, apparently written during harvest, describe vividly the unfaithfulness of Israel, using the figures of the wife unfaithful to her husband and of the joyous harvest feast turned to mourning. In these chapters we have the continuation of the same earnest appeal for repentance and an expression of a deep desire to bless, but the people are unmoved.

The next three chapters represent God's love for Israel in an exceedingly beautiful way. In a manner that should have touched the hardest heart Hosea reminded his people that God was both a God of mercy and a God of judgment. The picture in the eleventh chapter is that of a father who taught his child to walk and when the child became weary took him in his arms and carried him. Thus he reminded Israel of her dependence upon God and appealed for a surrender to his will and purpose as an absolute essential to the establishment of a relationship which alone God could bless.

Had the prophet been willing to close his message with the thirteenth chapter the end would have been an exceedingly dark one, and as we shall see presently the end of Israel's national life was tragically dark, but it did not have to be so. The fourteenth chapter is a final appeal to her to repent, with promise. It should be noted that while most prophecies include severe judgment for sin, there are no situations so dark that a ray of hope does not break through somewhere. As a matter of fact, Israel fell to the Assyrians less than a quarter of a century after the prophecy was concluded, but it was not inevitable that she should have done so. She was given an abundant opportunity to claim the promises of God through repentance. Her fall to the Assyrians in 722 B.C. and the removal of her people to a foreign country led to the loss of her national identity. Since that time she has been referred to as the ten lost tribes of Israel.

Hosea's message of judgment and love reflects a sympathy and an understanding superior to that of any other prophecy, due in part to the fact that he belonged to the Northern Kingdom (Israel) and as such expected to share with his people the tragedy or the blessings that would come, depending upon their response to God's claim for their allegiance.

JOEL—THE PROPHET OF HOPE

Outline

I. A DESCRIPTION OF DESTRUCTION. 1:1-12
    A. Destruction by the plague of locusts. 1:2-4
    B. Destruction by a nation. 1:5-7
    C. The call to mourn. 1:8-12

II. TWO DISTINCT CALLS TO REPENTANCE. 1:13—2:17
    A. Addressed to priests, and to people. 1:13-20
        1. For the Day of Jehovah is at hand. 1:13-17
        2. The beasts suffer pathetically. 1:18-20
    B. Addressed to all inhabitants of the land. 2:1-17
        1. A time of affliction. 2:1-11
        2. The offer of hope even now. 2:12-17

III. THE RESULT OF REPENTANCE. 2:18-27
    A. Return of prosperity; removal of enemy. 2:18-20
    B. Renewal of seasons and harvests. 2:21-27

IV. THE PROMISE OF A BRIGHTER FUTURE. 2:28—3:21
    A. The outpouring of God's Spirit. 2:28-32
    B. Israel's enemies are to be judged, after the return from exile. 3:1-17
        1. For breaking up the land.
        2. For commercializing humanity.
    C. Judah shall have material prosperity; her enemies are to be made desolate. 3:18-21

Comments

For an interesting discussion of the authorship, date, and unity of the book one should read carefully the Bible dictionary and the commentary. It will be seen that Joel was once considered the earliest of the minor prophecies and that now most scholars are agreed that it was written very late. There is general agreement that it was written by Joel, about whom we know almost nothing, and that the content shows a high degree of unity.

The book opens with an account of a series of pests which destroy vegetation and bring the inhabitants of the land, as well as the animals, into a state of dire need. The series of invading pests are probably different forms of the same general species. Their destructive powers are described as unusually complete and irresistible. While it is generally believed that the prophet meant to describe an actual event in the life of the people of Palestine, it is also agreed that this, even though exceedingly tragic, is but a foreshadowing of a more severe visitation known as the Day of the Lord.

In accordance with the common belief of his day, Joel saw in the plague of locusts evidences of the sins of his nation, and so he takes it for granted that his people have been guilty of sins for which God is sending upon them a visitation. He therefore calls on them to repent, without apparently having any specific transgressions in mind. The appeal is first to the priests and the people announcing that the Day of the Lord is at hand, and then as though he might not have been sufficiently inclusive he repeats the call, addressing all the inhabitants of the land (2:1) and assuring them of hope if they will repent (2:12-13).

There are those who think much time must have elapsed between the close of the seventeenth verse of the second chapter and the beginning of the eighteenth. This is on the assumption that the prophet had witnessed the fulfillment of the promise to those who repent. It is probably true that there had been a return of prosperity, removal of their enemies, and renewal of harvests and seasons, but history has not yet recorded the fulfillment of the twice-repeated statement, "And my people shall never be put to shame." (2:26-27.)

The prophet's vision for the future of his people reaches its climax in verses 28-32. Here he forsees the outpouring of God's Spirit upon all flesh. The passage closes with a positive reference to the remnant. This is a conception which many of the prophecies include. It is based upon the fundamental belief that God made a covenant with Abraham which has not yet been fulfilled but which, in the providence of God, is sure to come to pass. One cannot understand prophecy unless he realizes that back of much of the hope reflected in the Scriptures of the Old Testament is the assurance on the part of the inspired writer that the Messiah will surely come.

There is something strangely different about the prophecy of Joel from that of most other prophecies. He seems to have no conception of God's blessings being bestowed upon any peoples other than the Hebrews. His prophecy of utter judgment upon the Gentiles seems exceedingly harsh. There are those who have judged this prophecy severely because of this. He has been spoken of as a legalist and exceedingly narrow on the matter of race. Another has reminded us that Jesus in his prayer recorded in the seventeenth chapter of John uttered at one point a petition exclusively for his disciples. It is suggested that at this particular time Joel was justified in thinking exclusively of his own people. It is a bit difficult to believe, however, that the writer had in mind the development of a people who would be used to reach the multitudes, as was true of Jesus when he prayed exclusively for his disciples. A good case can be made for the justification of severe penalties upon the Gentiles because of their activity in breaking up the land, and their traffic in humanity for commerical purposes, but by the same processes of reasoning we have little difficulty in understanding why Judah might have been punished instead of blessed. It was only by the grace of God that Joel's own people were given the assurance of ultimate blessing.

The prophecy closes with the contrasting note of Judah's material prosperity and the destruction of her enemies, doubtless an occasion of rejoicing for those whose only concern was for one group of people, and who even felt a sense of satisfaction in the sufferings of all other peoples.

The last verse, "And I will cleanse their blood, that I have not cleansed: for the LORD dwelleth in Zion," seems a bit out of place here. There have been several interpretations of it. In view of his apparently narrow attitude on the race matter and the fact that he probably wrote as a contemporary of Ezra who was extremely zealous to break up the intermarriage of Jews and Gentiles, we wonder if he was not insisting upon the purity of the Hebrew race. But whatever our interpretation may be, we find Joel ending his prophecy with the reassuring note, "for the Lord dwelleth in Zion."

Amos—The Prophet of Justice

Outline

I. Divine Judgments Declared. Chapters 1—2
   A. Upon the Gentiles: Damascus, Gaza, Tyre, Edom, Ammon, and Moab. 1:3—2:3
   B. Upon Judah. 2:4-5
   C. Upon Israel. 2:6-8
   D. Israel severely rebuked. 2:9-16
      1. They are reminded of God's mercies. 2:9-12
      2. Their punishment described. 2:13-16

II. Three Discourses Introduced by "Hear This Word." Chapters 3—6
   A. The beginning of doom. 3:1-15
      1. Because Israel has been unfaithful. 3:1-12
      2. The day of visitation described. 3:13-15
   B. Woes to oppressors of poor and needy. 4:1-13
      1. The rich women rebuked. 4:1-3
      2. Israel's love for ritual and sacrifices. 4:4-5
      3. God's judgments have been ignored. 4:6-11
      4. "Prepare to meet thy God." 4:12-13
   C. The final doom of Israel. Chapters 5—6
      1. God's lamentation and appeal for repentance. 5:1-9
      2. Emptiness of unjust gain; call to better life. 5:10-15
      3. Lamentation, wailing, judgment. 5:16-27
      4. The rebuke of selfishness and insincerity; the assurance of destruction. 6:1-14

III. Five Visions with Interludes. 7:1—9:6
   A. Disasters in nature. 7:1-6
      1. Locusts—ended through Amos' intercession. 7:1-3
      2. Fire—ended through Amos' intercession. 7:4-6
   B. Of a more personal character. 7:7—9:6
      1. The plumbline. 7:7-9
      2. Interlude—encounter with Amaziah. 7:10-17

      3. Basket of summer fruit. 8:1-3

      4. Interlude—rebuke of people; prophecy of disaster. 8:4-14

      5. The Lord smites the altar. 9:1-6

IV. PROMISES—A LIGHT OUT OF THE DARKNESS. 9:7-15

    A. The house of Jacob remembered. 9:7-10

    B. Tabernacle of David raised up—Israel brought back. 9:11-15

Comments

Most scholars are agreed that Amos is not only the first of the minor prophecies but the first prophecy to have been written. There were prophets before Amos, but they apparently left no writings. He was probably the first to announce the Day of Jehovah about which we hear much from later writers.

As in all other studies in this series the student will gain much by careful reading of the commentary and the Bible dictionary as helps in the understanding of the biblical text. In these you will find illuminating statements helpful in understanding an ancient document couched in language imagery not always familiar to the twentieth-century student of the Scriptures.

The vigorous and almost harsh style of Amos is in striking contrast to that of Hosea. It will be remembered that Hosea was speaking to his own people with whom he would probably suffer as a result of the divine judgment passed upon them. Not so with Amos. He came from the Southern Kingdom and did not plan to remain in the north but a very short time. His was a passionate plea for justice and righteousness, which are closely related—"But let justice roll down as waters, and righteousness as a mighty stream." (5:24.)

The first two chapters are devoted to an announcement of divine judgments upon Gentile peoples and upon Judah and Israel. It is interesting to note that he opened his message with the pronouncement of judgment upon the age-old enemies of Israel and probably aroused them to a peak of enthusiasm when he declared that Judah also would be judged. This was a carefully devised strategy to make his message to Israel the more effective when he not only included them among those whom God would punish, but sternly rebuked them and with vividness described the severity with which they would be punished.

The second section contains the main body of the prophecy arranged in three separate discourses, each of which is opened with the statement, "Hear this word" or "Hear ye this word." The first (chapter 3) deals with the beginning of their doom, which came about a quarter of a century after he spoke. It is clearly stated that the divine visitation would be the result of Israel's unfaithfulness. The description of the day of visitation reflects the prophet's abhorrence of Israel's desecration of the true worship of God and the fact that so many of her people were living in luxury at the expense of those who were helplessly poor.

The second discourse (chapter 4) carries forward the rebuke of the well-to-do who oppress the poor and needy. Special mention is made of the lavish luxury in which many of the women live. Amos likens them to the fat cattle of Bashan. Apparently they had pressed their husbands to severe practices of oppression. These, Amos assures them, will not escape the judgment. Verses 4 and 5 should be read together. The full force of this passage will be seen when the reader ponders well the phrase, "For this pleaseth you." In the paragraph which follows, the prophet seems to be saying that God has visited them with many judgments in the hope that they would return to him, but to no avail. Then come those memorable words, "Prepare to meet thy God."

The third discourse is opened with the variant wording, "Hear ye this word," adding the word "ye" for effect as he declares their final doom. A careful reading of this section (chapters 5 and 6), following the outline above, will probably be sufficient to make clear what it is the prophet was trying to say to Israel.

The third section, consisting of five visions, falls naturally into two divisions: disasters in nature, and those of a more personal character. We are familiar with the plague of locusts referred to in other sections of the Bible. The fire is probably the prophet's vivid way of describing a devastating drought which so completely dried up all vegetation that the earth's surface had the appearance of having been burned over.

The plumbline of righteousness reveals the extent to which Israel had departed from her God and indicates that she is in immediate danger of being destroyed. The encounter with Amaziah is most revealing. (7:10-17.) Summer fruits are in many respects the most seasonal of all vegetation. A basket of summer fruits (those which have been plucked from the tree) remain good but a little while. We have in this vision, therefore, a clear indication that Israel's doom is not far off. The style of the writer leaves no doubt in the mind of the reader about the underlying reasons for God's judgment upon Israel, neither is there uncertainty as to what the punishment will be. (8:4-14.) The last vision, the most tragic of all, vividly describes the extent of her destruction. (9:1-6.)

Verses 7 to 15 of the ninth chapter seem almost like an afterthought on the part of the prophet. When we remember, however, that he is deeply conscious of the covenant of God with Abraham we cannot see how he could have concluded his message with the sixth verse. A remnant shall be left!

OBADIAH—THE PROPHET OF JUDGMENT UPON EDOM

Outline

I. EDOM'S PERIL. VSS. 1-9
  A. The Lord's condemnation of pride. Vss. 1-4
  B. Edom's lack of security. Vss. 5-9

II. EDOM'S GUILT AND JUDGMENT. VSS. 10-16
  A. Her sin against a brother. Vss. 10-14
  B. "The day of Jehovah is near." Vss. 15-16

III. ISRAEL'S RESTORATION; EDOM'S DOOM. VSS. 17-21
  A. Israel's triumph. Vss. 17-18
  B. Esau's destruction. Vss. 19-21

Comments

The opening verse of this, the shortest book in the Old Testament, gives a clue to what to expect: "Thus saith the Lord GOD concerning Edom." The Edomites were descendants of Esau. The entire story is reminiscent of a feud between twin brothers, Jacob and Esau. While there were times when they seemed to express for each other a brotherly spirit, the dominant relationship had been that of bitter hatred.

As will be seen from a study of your Bible, the Bible dictionary, and the commentary, this is an exceedingly difficult book to understand. There are those who say that it does not contain a spiritual lesson. Dummelow's commentary states an exceedingly unworthy purpose for its having been written which the writer is unwilling to accept. The statement in the dictionary is far more acceptable. Calkins in his book, *The Modern Messages of the Minor Prophets,* says, "The book consists of a shriek of rage, a shout of defiance, a cry of victory." Such a characterization is acceptable when rightly understood. Further reference will be made to this later.

Those who see in the book nothing but racial hatred must look deeper. The first two sections (see preceding outline) may very well be taken as an expression of divine disapproval of sin wherever it is found. In this case the sin happens to have been committed against Israel. In the first place, the condemnation is aimed against Edom because of her pride and her dependence on her own resources for security. In the second place, Edom's sin against her brother in time of need certainly holds for us a tremendous message today. Apparently she was not even aggressive in the time of Israel's adversity but rejoiced in it, and what is more, she did not raise her voice in protest. If we press these words very far in a modern-day application we may be face to face with what might easily become a severe test of our own faithfulness in protesting evils which we see all about us. In every community we are conscious of evils which are bringing hardships to our fellow men, and like Edom we are doing nothing to correct the conditions. Read again verses 10-14.

The third section, describing the triumph of Israel and the destruction of Edom, is subject to the criticism of an undue pride for one's own race and bitter prejudice for another race. It may be that such an emphasis affected too greatly the spirit of the writer, but it does not necessarily preclude the fact that we have here the expression of something infinitely deeper. It is for this that we must look if the prophecy is to have a spiritual significance for us.

The prophet, regardless of his identity, was surely conscious that the God in whose name he wrote had many times visited his people, Israel, with punishment because of their sins. He cannot have thought that God cared only for Israel. The Old Testament is replete with evidences of his care for others.

There is reason to believe that the message of the book rests firmly upon a fundamental conception of God's righteousness and the consequent relation which all mankind must sustain to him. It is worthy of mention that in the beginning of the ancient feud God made choice between an idealism expressed by Jacob and the mundane attitude of his brother Esau. Having begun at that point it is clear that in choosing Jacob over his brother, God did not approve of all that Jacob was and did.

Dr. Calkins takes the position, with which the writer is in accord, that the two men and the two groups which descended from them symbolized something of fundamental importance, namely an acceptance of God's righteousness and man's subservience to him, and the baser attitude that would lead one to forfeit a birthright to satisfy a temporary sense of need. It is true that the descendants of Jacob did not measure up to the idealism expressed, but throughout their long history there was at least a remnant that remained true to the faith. The record seems to indicate that the Edomites were equally true to the attitude of their father Esau.

From this point of view the prophecy of Obadiah is tremendously significant. Even though sternly stated, it is the reaffirmation of the prophet's faith that there are two warring forces in the hearts and lives of individuals and groups, and that ultimately the one will triumph and the other will be destroyed. Such a faith is abundantly justified by the Scriptures as a whole, and is faithfully restated in this prophecy.

Jonah—The Prophet of Outreach

Outline

I. Resistance. Chapter 1
    A. Jonah tries to escape a command. 1:1-3
    B. The storm. 1:4-10
    C. The storm subsides. 1:11-17

II. REPENTANCE. Chapter 2
   A. The cry of distress. 2:1-3
   B. Prayer of confession. 2:4-8
   C. Rededication. 2:9-10

III. Return. Chapter 3
   A. A second commission to preach. 3:1-2
   B. Jonah's response. 3:3-4
   C. Nineveh's response to his preaching. 3:5-10

IV. REBELLION. Chapter 4
   A. The sulking prophet. 4:1-5
   B. The parable of the gourd. 4:6-11

Comments

It is unfortunate that the book of Jonah, of such great value to sacred literature, should have been so badly obscured by the story of the fish. This should never have occupied the central place in the thinking of the reader. It is generally agreed, regardless of what one thinks of the miraculous element involved, that the outstanding message of the prophecy is of a missionary nature—God commanded his spokesman to carry the message to a people who were not Jews.

As such the message of this book is in striking contrast to an interpretation of Obadiah which makes the prophet magnify the Hebrew people and decry the Gentiles. The two books illustrate well the fact that to understand Scripture the reader must be careful to discover just what the author's major emphasis is in a given passage.

The student will do well to study the Westminster Bible dictionary article, where he will find a carefully prepared statement regarding the two interpretations of the story as a whole, indicating that there are those who regard the narrative as a literal description of an experience of a prophet of the Lord, while others consider it an allegory similar to the parables of Jesus. The latter position seems to be the one held by the writer of the commentary on this book. Apart from the virtues of the separate positions it will be seen that all are agreed that the message is the same; namely, God has a message for all peoples, and Israel has been chosen as the human agent through whom that message should be proclaimed.

The behavior of the missionary—Jonah—reveals traits of human nature recognizable in every generation. It is nothing short of amazing that one should feel a definite sense of call to the prophetic ministry and resist so vigorously a clear call to a particular mission. More amazing still is the fact that, having preached reluctantly, Jonah should have been so bitterly rebellious at the effectiveness of his preaching. Over against all this is the fact that one with such a spirit could be used of God to accomplish his purposes.

Since there are so many available helps which emphasize the missionary message of the book it may be well in this brief discussion to deal with the outstanding characteristics of the missionary whose spirit reflects too well, unfortunately, the experiences of multitudes of religious leaders who have come after him.

The outline indicates that there were four R's which characterize his total experience as reflected in the book: Resistance, Repentance, Return, and Rebellion. Resistance to the call to preach the gospel has probably been the most characteristic experience of the young men who have entered the gospel ministry, and probably the impulse of many a one who never yielded to the call. The experience of repentance, the rededication of life, and entering upon the ministry have usually followed; few have ever experienced such signal success as that which followed the preaching of Jonah. And what can we say more? Have any been rebellious at the results which have come to us? As a matter of fact, it may be that too few of us have had the courage of Jonah to preach in all of its fullness the message that is ours, simply because we feared what might happen if we did. There is in the gospel message that which would revolutionize society if it were preached effectively. There is still an unwillingness to preach the whole gospel with all its implications for society.

It is essentially unfair to assume that the experience of Jonah should be considered as having its parallel only in the lives of those who have been called to preach. There are literally thousands of lay men and lay women who have a sense of call to Christian service. This group have also had similar experiences in their challenge to serve in various activities of the church, the home, and the community. In the midst of the preparation to write this brief statement the writer was delightfully interrupted by one who feels a compelling urge to express in her own life a conviction, to pull out from her place in her own group and take a stand upon the grounds of a higher idealism, and to assume a leadership vastly different from that of her upbringing. The deterrent influence inheres in the cost of such a procedure. The right course seems clear. The terrific strain emerges at the point of what such a break will cost and whether or not it is ultimately worth while.

If a prophet such as Jonah could, as an instrument in the hands of God, effect such a transformation in a vast multitude, how much more may one whose spirit is in harmony with the spirit of his Maker achieve in this day of unprecedented challenge!

MICAH—THE PROPHET OF JUSTICE AND LOVE

Outline

I. HEAR YE—ALL PEOPLES. Chapters 1—2
   A. Judgment of Samaria and Judah. 1:1-16
   B. Woes declared to the wicked oppressors. 2:1-11
   C. A remnant will be left. 2:12-13

II. HEAR YE—RELIGIOUS AND POLITICAL LEADERS. Chapters 3—5
   A. Indictment because of lack of justice. 3:1-12
   B. Future exaltation of God's kingdom. 4:1—5:1
   C. A Deliverer shall come from Bethlehem. 5:2-15

III. "HEAR YE NOW WHAT THE LORD SAITH." Chapters 6—7
   A. Jehovah's reiteration of mercies. 6:1-5
   B. Requirements of true religion. 6:6-8
   C. Moral corruption prevails instead. 6:9—7:6
   D. The prophet's confidence in God. 7:7-20

Comments

Someone has said of the prophet Micah that he had Amos' passion for justice and Hosea's heart of love. A review of the discussions of these prophecies will show the validity of this statement.

Apparently Samaria is on the threshold of her destruction. After a description of the resulting desolation, Micah predicts a similar experience for Jerusalem, the fulfillment of which is probably a century removed from the time of his writing. There is much political unrest, and with Samaria out of the way the Assyrians, the dominant world power of that time, would apparently have easy access to the Southern Kingdom. Isaiah tells us that the king of Judah agreed to pay heavy tribute to Assyria and thus put off the evil day of her own destruction, which did not actually occur until the Babylonian Empire came into power.

The sins for which Israel and Samaria were to be punished are vividly described and are the occasion for great lamentation. The extremes to which people resorted as an expression of lament seem incomprehensible to us, but were doubtless used to dramatize outwardly an inner state of mind and heart.

The declaration of woes against the wicked are accompanied by terrifying descriptions of the extent to which people went to defraud and oppress the weak. Evil devices are carefully planned in the early hour of the morning and are executed "when the morning is light." The seizure of ordinary property does not satisfy; they go beyond that and take "even a man and his heritage." The heritage here referred to had more than ordinary significance to people of those days. But worse, they invaded the sanctities of home life—"The women of my people ye cast out from their pleasant houses; from their young children ye take away my glory for ever." (2:9.) Possibly women and children were being sold into foreign captivity. More likely, the reference is to the breakdown of home life that is an aftermath of war.

In verse 12 the remnant is mentioned. The plot never gets so dark as to obscure for the prophet the assurance that there will be a small group through whom the covenant with Abraham will be preserved. It is worthy of note that in each of the three sections there is that gleam of hope following the terror of divine judgment.

The first section of the book was an appeal to all peoples. The second section is addressed to the religious and political leaders who have been responsible for the extreme abuses of their day. The prophet severely rebukes them for having sunk to the low estate evidenced by their spirit and their conduct. Here we cannot but accept with a real sense of chagrin the fact that through the centuries, and even now, the religious and political leaders have been too largely responsible for the evils which have been, and are, so prevalent in society. It is but another way of saying that those who have won the confidence of the people have forfeited the right to lead and thus have brought sorrow and suffering to multitudes.

In the first paragraph of the fourth chapter we have the vision of a time when there will be no more war. This is indicated by the prophecy that implements of war will be transformed into implements of agriculture. The second paragraph declares that God will accomplish his purpose through a faithful remnant—"I will gather that which is driven away, and that which I have afflicted." The last paragraph probably refers to the Babylonian exile and the return from captivity.

The fifth chapter is one of the most loved chapters in all the Old Testament because it not only foretells the birth of Christ but the place he is to be born. Here it is that Micah gives expression to one of his greatest passions, namely the exaltation of the humble and the lowly. He seems to have been deeply concerned about the interests of that mass of people in every generation who belong to the poorer classes and hence can do little for themselves. In this passage, of course, we have a magnificent expression of the ultimate triumph of the Kingdom of God.

The last section of the book is an appeal to the people to hear what Jehovah has to say. It is true that Micah has all along been speaking in the name of God, but here he is doubly emphatic that it is Jehovah who speaks. The outline is probably all that one needs as a guide to an understanding of the message. The reiteration of God's mercies contains beautiful and tender expressions of the love of a father for his children. (6:1-5; 7:18-20.) The first part of the second paragraph may be interpreted as the cry of a disturbed people who are willing to do anything to please God. On the other hand, it may be nothing more than a sarcastic retort to one whom they conceive to be unreasonable in his demands. In either event the answer is fitting: "He hath showed thee, O man, what is good; and what doth the LORD require of thee, but to do justly, and to love kindness, and to walk humbly with thy God?"

"What doth God require of thee?" This is not too simple when one realizes that the prophet is, in the paragraph which follows, explaining the meaning of "do justly" and "love kindness." He is clearly saying that it must affect every human relationship, including business transactions of all kinds.

Chapter 7 indicates that confession and repentance are the only source of hope. (7:9.)

God who called his people out of Egypt will again "show unto them marvelous things" and work out his purposes through them.

The last paragraph is an expression of Micah's confidence in the future. Again he is resting the case of his hope upon the covenant with Abraham. Read verse 20.

NAHUM—THE PROPHET OF JUDGMENT AGAINST ASSYRIA

Outline

I. JUDGMENT UPON NINEVEH ANNOUNCED. Chapter 1
    A. Judgment by a sovereign God. 1:1-8
    B. Judgment upon a wicked counselor. 1:9-14
    C. Reassurance to Judah. 1:15

II. THE EXECUTION OF JUDGMENT. Chapter 2
    A. The fierce siege described. 2:1-10
    B. A taunt and a prophecy. 2:11-13

III. REASONS FOR THE JUDGMENT. Chapter 3
    A. Sins of oppression. 3:1-3
    B. Sins of infidelity. 3:4-7
    C. Doom inevitable; Nineveh not better than No-Amon. 3:8-19

Comments

This prophecy is distinctly aimed at the Assyrian nation which for a long period of time had been a dominant world power, and in her relation to weaker nations an exceedingly ruthless people. One may regard Nahum as in some sense a supplement to the book of Jonah, though it is written from an entirely different point of view and with an entirely different outcome.

Few prophecies are more clearly dated than this one. The fall of ancient Thebes is referred to and we know that this took place in 663 B.C., and Nineveh the capital city of Assyria is clearly standing at the time of the writing, though her doom seems imminent. Nineveh did not fall until 612 B.C. A conflict between Assyria and Babylonia in 626 B.C. marked a definite turning point in Nineveh's power of empire. It is generally agreed that the prophecy was written between 625 and 612 B.C. There are some scholars who think it was written about 614 B.C.

Little is known about the writer himself. He clearly reveals a conviction of the sovereignty of God, his ultimate triumph over unrighteousness, and the vindication of his covenant made with Abraham. Nahum is a prophet of the country of Judah, but makes little reference to her. The one thing that is uppermost in his mind and heart is that Assyria, for long the adversary of his people, but more especially the adversary of the things that are right, must cease to dominate the peoples of the then known world.

In presenting the above outline the writer is keenly conscious, as he is in the presentation of all outlines in this study, that there are many textual problems which such outlines seem to disregard. For example, there are those who think that the first chapter of Nahum was written by another author about the year 300 B.C. Whether this is true or not, the message of the chapter is in harmony with the purpose of the writer and his conception of the ultimate subservience of all peoples to the power and purpose of Almighty God.

If one will read the first chapter with the outline before him he will be able to see the connection. The wicked counselor probably refers to the military powers of Assyria who were more like dictators than counselors. The fifteenth verse of the first chapter and the second verse of chapter 2 may well be read together as containing a message of reassurance to Judah.

The seige described in the opening verses of the second chapter is strikingly like those which Assyria had made time and again. Now she is being faced with the contemplation of a military force which will ultimately bring her to her knees. The second section of this chapter contains two distinct elements, a taunt and a prophecy. The first reads appallingly like the exultation of one who stands by and rejoices in the suffering of another. This discordant note has been the occasion for some to question the purity of the text at this point. More about this later. The prophecy of Nineveh's ultimate judgment is clear.

Many students of this book combine the second and third chapters under the general heading of judgment. Yet there seems to be some justification for making a second division, because in the third chapter there are certain definite reasons set forth for the judgment visited, or to be visited, upon Nineveh. It is here that we begin to get the picture of the ruthlessness with which the Assyrians had, through a long period of time, treated weak and helpless peoples.

The sins of oppression are vividly defined. The language is so frank and so blunt that there are those who have questioned the right of the book to a place in the canon of Holy Scriptures. Another reminds us that our practice of using polite language for crude behavior tends to weaken for us and for others the true meaning of that about which we speak. However we may want to interpret the language, it is there in its stark reality, giving us a picture of a condition which must ultimately be dealt with by a just God.

At this point (3:1-7) the outline may be in error. It will be noted that it breaks a paragraph, describing the first part of it as having to do with sins of oppression, and the second part with sins of infidelity. In whatever way they are taken they refer to a quality of heart and mind and a practice of life in relation to other peoples which are expressive of a situation that not only justifies the condemnation of God but demands it.

The last section reminds Nineveh that she is no better than No-Amon (Thebes), nor is she better fortified against a successful attack by another, and yet No-Amon fell. At some length the writer tells of her doom and the contempt in which she will be held by the nations around her. There are those who have challenged the right of the last verse to be included as a part of the inspired Word of God on the assumption that this is clearly an expression of personal hate. We may be reminded here that Nahum wrote before there was much said about loving our enemies. Another has pointed out the justification of the vindictive spirit when it is in support of the triumph of righteousness over evil.

HABAKKUK—THE PHILOSOPHER

Outline

I. THE HUMAN-DIVINE DIALOGUE. 1:1—2:4
    A. The prophet pleads for justice. 1:1-4
    B. God's dramatic reply. 1:5-11
    C. The prophet sees dimly. 1:12-17
    D. The prophet looks to God and is reassured. 2:1-4

II. FIVE WOES AGAINST THE ENEMY. 2:5-20
    A. Whose ambition is unlawful gain. 2:5-14
    B. Because of deceitfulness and violence. 2:15-17
    C. Who worship dumb, lifeless idols. 2:18-20

III. A PSALM AND A PRAYER. 3:1-19.
    A. The mingled expressions of fear and adoration. 3:1-16
    B. A sense of assurance and triumph. 3:17-19

Comments

There is perhaps no book in the Old Testament of comparable significance to Habakkuk which is so little read and so imperfectly understood. About the prophet we know nothing except what we have in the brief volume of three short chapters. Apparently he wrote between the time that the Babylonian Empire came into power and the destruction of Jerusalem—between 612 and 586 B.C. Most scholars believe that he wrote near the turn of the century at a time when the status of Judah was so uncertain and when the armies of Babylonia had already begun to threaten her existence.

The first section of this prophecy is composed of a human-divine dialogue which is concluded with the fourth verse of the second chapter. Here the prophet is deeply concerned about the apparent injustices of life and in a forthright manner challenges God to show where he is wrong in the belief that justice has not been extended to the people and that God himself is responsible for this deplorable situation. This is a record of prophet, whose commission is to speak for God to the people, having reversed the procedure and boldly spoken to God for the people.

The answer which God gave him as contained in verses 5-11 describes vividly a bitter and hasty nation waiting on the border, as it were, to swoop down upon Judah and ruthlessly destroy her. As a matter of fact, if our dating of the book is correct that very thing was about to happen. Surely there was not much consolation in this, so the prophet seeks for an understanding of why such a thing could be.

At this point there begins to break through the confusion of mind a glimmer of light. The key to the situation is seen in the twelfth verse, where the prophet exclaims: "O LORD, thou hast ordained him for judgment; and thou, O Rock, hast established him for correction." Having arrived at the conclusion that Judah's military defeat was for judgment and correction he comes face to face with the age-old question: Why is it that the wicked triumph over those who are more righteous than they? This, indeed, is the point of his greatest difficulty. It is the riddle of life that has disturbed multitudes of people in every generation.

The really great decision is made when the prophet determines to turn aside in quiet and patient meditation to wait and see what the ultimate answer to his questions will be, and for this answer he looks to God.

Presently the answer came, and it was this: "For the vision is yet for the appointed time, and it hasteth toward the end, and shall not lie: though it tarry, wait for it; because it will surely come, it will not delay. Behold, his soul is puffed up, it is not upright in him; but the righteous shall live by his faith." A tremendously reassuring answer because it carried with it the fundamental conception of the ultimate triumph of right as a true expression of God's goodness and justice. The delay was disappointing, for the prophet apparently had hoped to live to see the triumph of righteousness but now it was quite clear that the divinely appointed time would not be in his day.

Having arrived at a clearer understanding of the providences of

God, the prophet is in a position to speak with assurance regarding the enemy—not only Judah's enemies but the enemies of the eternal purposes of God himself. Thus in the remaining section of the second chapter the prophet announces five woes which may be arranged in three general classifications as indicated in the outline. The Revised Standard Version devotes a paragraph to each of the woes described.

The striking difference between the spirit of the first and third chapters of this little book is exceedingly revealing. In the first there are evidences of bitterness and impatience; in the third there is a resigned, but not a defeated, spirit—a resignation which has in it the note of joy and triumph felt by one who has discovered the will and purpose of God. Even though he does not expect to share in its ultimate realization, he rejoices nevertheless.

Many are those who found in Habakkuk comfort and hope during the tragic years of World War II. Perhaps few prayers taken from the Old Testament expressed more perfectly the deep yearning of the human heart than the prophet's cry: "O Lord revive thy work in the midst of the years; in the midst of the years make it known; in wrath remember mercy." *In wrath remember mercy!*

This prophecy illustrates well a characteristic of the Hebrew prophet who saw clearly the will and purpose of God, and who proclaimed it fearlessly and with a spirit of rejoicing because he knew it to be true, even though the immediate providences were to be severe and the occasion of bitterness. He could look beyond his own pleasures and comforts and rejoice that in God's own time unborn generations would be the recipients of his goodness and his mercy.

ZEPHANIAH—THE PROPHET OF UNIVERSAL JUDGMENT

Outline

I. A UNIVERSAL JUDGMENT. Chapter 1
    A. Including Judah and Jerusalem. 1:1-6
    B. The Day of Jehovah at hand (utter destruction). 1:7-18

II. EXHORTATION TO SEEK GOD; SPECIFIC JUDGMENTS. 2:1—3:8
    A. Hope for those who have kept his ordinances. 2:1-3

    B. Judgment on many neighbors. 2:4-15
    C. Judgment on Jerusalem. 3:1-8

III. A REMNANT SHALL BE BLESSED. 3:9-20
    A. A remnant maintained its integrity and was blessed. 3:9-13
    B. The ultimate triumph of the righteous. 3:14-20

Comments

In contrast with many writers of prophecy we have information about Zephaniah which connects him with the top leadership of his day and several generations preceding him. He was a contemporary of Jeremiah and was probably one of those who influenced the young king Josiah to make reforms in the interest of religion. Apparently he was a young man who wrote at the very beginning of the rise of the Babylonian Empire to power.

There is no prophecy which is more clearly characterized by the word "Judgment" than is this one. After telling us who the writer is, the narrative moves immediately and swiftly to proclaim universal judgment, including that of Judah and Jerusalem. Someone has said that Zephaniah lacked the note of sympathetic understanding which is evident in Hosea and Micah because he came from a well-to-do group who did not know the trials and disappointments of poor people.

Since this study has retained the order of the books as they appear in the Bible we may miss the force of some statements. For example, while one or two prophets had had something to say about the Day of Jehovah it was a comparatively new thought at the time Zephaniah wrote. He pictured the tragic and utter darkness of this day as no other writer has done.

It may be a more or less arbitrary choice to make a break in the outline following chapter 1. It is fitting that having painted a severely dark picture the prophet should inject the note of hope if there was any reason to believe mercy might be shown. The first three verses of chapter 2 are obviously a call to repentance, regardless of who may be addressed. Apparently Isaiah and Amos used similar ways of indicating it. It is quite clear that hope is held out to those who have kept God's ordinances and who will seek after him. The only avenue that even a righteous man has to God is through repentance.

A large number of Judah's neighbors upon whom judgments were pronounced are little more than names to us. To the contemporaries of Zephaniah, however, they were exceedingly meaningful. Some had been her enemies and others had been her allies.

The reader may question the warrant for indicating that in 3:1-8 the prophet is specifying Jerusalem. The immediate context would seem to support this position. The marginal references reveal that Jerusalem was referred to by others in the use of language similar to the descriptive language of this passage.

Many scholars believe that Zephaniah did not write verses 9-20, but that it was a much later addition appended to lessen the terrific force of the most severe pronouncements of judgment recorded anywhere in biblical literature. It should be observed that even so the passage may properly belong here. We have the witness of Scripture as a whole that while the prophets portray the shadowy side of life deliberately and frankly, painting it in its rugged reality, we are not left hopeless. The shafts of light break through the darkness not merely for effect or to please, but because of the very constitution of the universe by an all-wise and all-powerful God whose purposes are good and will ultimately be brought to a happy realization.

Verses 14-20 have been characterized by some as the finest section of the book. One wonders how much of it, if any, has yet been fulfilled. There has been a return from captivity, but can we be sure that the Babylonian captivity is all that is here meant? Verse 19 may have a warning in it for those who are anti-Semitic in spirit. When anti-Semitism was at its height in Germany under the Nazi rule, someone made the observation that the Jew had stood at the graveside of all his enemies. This concept may not properly be pushed too far, but there is clearly an element of truth here that should warn us against racial hatred.

HAGGAI—THE PROPHET OF RECONSTRUCTION

Outline

I. EXHORTATION TO BUILD THE HOUSE OF THE LORD. 1:1-15
   A. The Lord's word revealed by the prophet to the governor, the high priest, and the people. 1:1-2
   B. The Lord's rebuke to a people who had become wayward and selfish. 1:3-6
   C. A challenge to rebuild the Temple. 1:7-11
   D. The response. 1:12-15

II. EXPRESSIONS OF ENCOURAGEMENT. 2:1-9
   A. Comparison of old and new Temple. 2:1-5
   B. The Lord's promise of success. 2:6-9

III. REASONS WHY GOD'S BLESSING WAS WITHHELD. 2:10-19
   (Sequel to prophecy in 1:7-11)
   A. The unclean pollutes the clean—their neglect of God prevented his blessing. 2:10-17
   B. The result of revived zeal: ". . . from this day will I bless you." 2:18-19

IV. THE HOPES OF ISRAEL WILL YET BE REALIZED. 2:20-23
   (Sequel to prophecy in 2:1-9)
   A. The nations will be shaken. 2:20-22
   B. Zerubbabel will be established. 2:23

Comments

The prophecy of Haggai is more accurately dated than any of the others we have discussed. None other is so generally agreed to be the product of one author. Haggai is here dealing with one specific thing: namely, the rebuilding of the Temple of the Lord, a Temple which at this time had lain in ruins for nearly seventy years.

One cannot understand the situation regarding the rebuilding of the Temple without a familiarity with the first seven chapters of the book of Ezra. The story briefly stated is that when the remnant returned from their exile in 538 B.C., immediate steps were taken to re-establish the altar and to reconstruct the Temple. The Samaritans asked to have a part in the work and when refused that privilege set themselves immediately to thwart the purposes of the Hebrews and were successful in having the work stopped. For sixteen years nothing was done. Haggai and Zechariah, contemporary prophets, began a vigorous movement for the restoration and in an incredibly short time the work was completed.

After a brief statement introducing a new era the prophet launched upon a series of appeals which were amazingly effective. It is of interest to notice that the challenge made was responded to by the governor, the high priest, and all the people. The secret of the whole matter is stated in the fourteenth verse of the first chapter: "And the Lord stirred up the spirit of Zerubbabel the son of Shealtiel, governor of Judah, and the spirit of Joshua the son of Jehozadak, the high priest, and the spirit of all the remnant of the people; and they came and did work on the house of the Lord of hosts, their God."

The opening verses of the second chapter imply that there developed early in the work of rebuilding a keen sense of discouragement. To meet the challenge of that situation the prophet addressed a question to the people, asking: "Who is left among you that saw this house in its former glory? and how do ye see it now? is it not in your eyes as nothing?" (Vs. 3.) Verses 8 and 9 state a conviction on which he based his words of reassurance.

If there was anyone living at that time who remembered the former Temple, it is obvious that he or she was between eighty and ninety years of age. There are those who think the prophet implied that he himself saw the former Temple. It is certain that all of them had a vivid picture of what it was like, because the Hebrews were careful to keep alive in the minds of their children the days before disaster befell their sacred city.

It may be that Haggai had hoped that the governor of his time would be the one to usher in the Messianic age. There are many implications pointing to that conclusion. He probably lived long enough to discover that this fond dream would not come true in his lifetime.

His phrase in verse 11, "Ask now the priests concerning the law," has been interpreted to be an overemphasis upon a legalistic point of view. The words which follow in the same paragraph indicate the real meaning—holiness was not readily transmitted, but uncleanness was. Their neglect of God had rendered ineffectual all they undertook.

The message of Haggai, while definitely appealing for the rebuilding of the Temple, was far more than that. He was seeking the restoration of religion in the lives of the small and struggling group who at heart wanted that which religion provided. They had too long allowed themselves to be content with the commonplace and had become contaminated by the disintegrating influences of a secularism which had terribly affected their entire outlook on life.

Interpreted in this broader sense the book has a tremendously significant message for the church of the twentieth century. We need not think that because we do not face the building of a material Temple the book of Haggai is meaningless to us. He is dealing here with basic principles affecting the relationships of people with people, and that which relates all of humanity to God.

ZECHARIAH—THE PROPHET OF RECONSTRUCTION AND RE-ESTABLISHMENT

Outline of Chapters 1—8

I. A CALL TO REPENTANCE. 1:1-6

II. EIGHT VISIONS OF ENCOURAGEMENT. 1:7—6:8
    A. The colored horses. 1:7-17
       Sent by God; nations at rest; angel's appeal for God's mercy; God's jealousy for Zion and promise of blessing.
    B. The four horns and the four smiths. 1:18-21
       The horns have scattered Judah; the smiths are come to destroy the horns.
    C. The city without a wall. 2:1-13
       Jerusalem not to be restored on old foundations, a new day was dawning; many nations would turn to God; the announcement of prosperity for Zion.
    D. The high priest and Satan his accuser. 3:1-10
       Joshua, a brand plucked from the fire clothed in rags, must be cleansed and re-established. The restored priesthood is a pledge of the Messiah who will come.

E. The golden candlestick and two olive trees. 4:1-14

The word to Zerubbabel. (Vs. 6.) Zerubbabel began a good work; he shall finish it. The olive trees and branches are the anointed ones (Joshua and Zerubbabel—anointed priest and king). (Vs. 14.)

F. The flying roll. 5:1-4

This document represents a curse which goes out over the earth.

G. The woman in a barrel (ephah). 5:5-11

A sequel to the flying roll. Wickedness personified and removed.

H. The four chariots. 6:1-8

Represent the four winds—unseen powers of God used to protect his people against their enemies.

III. SYMBOLIC CROWNING OF HIGH PRIEST. 6:9-15

A. Joshua of the Old Testament is Jesus of the New Testament. The proclamation of the Messiah. 6:9-14

B. New recruits for the building of the Temple. 6:15

IV. INQUIRY CONCERNING FASTS. 7:1—8:23

A. Fasting is not unto God. 7:1-7. (Cf. Isa. 1:11-12; I Cor. 8:8.)

B. God requires justice and kindness. 7:8-14

C. God will return to Zion. 8:1-17

1. He will restore and establish his people. 8:1-8
2. People who were once a curse among the nations will become a blessing. 8:9-13
3. He will bless his people, who are to live in truth, justice, peace. 8:14-17

D. Fasts shall become festivals. 8:18-23

Comments

The reader will recall that Zephaniah was a young man at the time he wrote and that his prophecy was an exceedingly gloomy one. There are those who have assumed that the dark picture he painted was the reflection of a characteristic of youth to be severe in attitude toward those who are evil. We now come to the work of another very young prophet whose writings reflect an extremely optimistic attitude toward the contemporary situation and what the future holds for its people.

A comparison of the prophecies of Zechariah and Haggai reveal at once that the authors were contemporaries and that the book of Haggai and the first eight chapters of Zechariah are closely related in that they seek the same ends; namely, the restoration of the Temple and so the re-establishing of religion to its rightful place in the lives of the Jews who had returned from the Babylonian captivity.

While this may be regarded as a companion volume to Haggai, it is perhaps more accurately characterized as supplementing it. However broadly we may interpret the eight visions they were certainly intended to be an encouragement to the discouraged group who had returned to the land of their fathers. See Bible dictionary and commentary for a detailed discussion of the visions.

The surface impression of the third vision—the city without a wall—does not do justice to its full meaning. Surely the prophet meant to say that the attitude which sought to restore her along the lines of the former city was fundamentally wrong. There is a tremendous message in this thought for our own day.

The fourth vision deals basically with re-establishing the priesthood which had necessarily been in disrepute for a long period of time due to the fact that Israel had been among an unclean people. In such a situation their religious practices were degraded—certainly from the point of view of the Jewish people. This is elaborated upon in 6:9-15. (Some believe this passage refers to the crowning of Zerubbabel rather than Joshua, but in either case the ultimate fulfillment is in Christ, the Branch. Compare Isa. 11:1.)

Those who are perplexed over the meaning of fasts and whether they have been neglected unduly will profit greatly by a careful study of the seventh and eighth chapters. The outline may be helpful.

Outline of Chapters 9—14

I. THE COMING OF THE MESSIANIC KINGDOM. 9:1—10:2
    A. Overthrow of hostile nations. 9:1-8
    B. The Messianic King. 9:9-10
    C. Promise of victory and freedom. 9:11-17
    D. The folly of superstition. 10:1-2

II. THE DESTRUCTION OF THE WORLD POWERS AND THE GATHERING OF DISPERSED ISRAEL. 10:3—11:3
    A. The victory. 10:3-7

B. The restoration. 10:8-12

C. The ruin of the hostile powers. 11:1-3

III. THE TWO SHEPHERDS, THE FAITHFUL AND THE FALSE. 11:4-17; 13:7-9
   A. The faithful shepherd. 11:4-14
   B. The false shepherd. 11:15-17

IV. THE HEATHEN ASSAULT UPON JERUSALEM. HER DELIVERANCE, PENITENCE, AND PURIFICATION. 12:1—13:6
   A. The assault and deliverance. 12:1-9
   B. Penitential mourning. 12:10-14
   C. Forgiveness and reformation. 13:1-6

V. THE FINAL ASSAULT UPON JERUSALEM. THE ISSUE IN THE UNIVERSAL RECOGNITION AND WORSHIP OF JEHOVAH AS KING. 14:1-21
   A. Jehovah fights against the heathen assailants of Jerusalem. 14:1-5
   B. Climate and scenery miraculously transformed. 14:6-11
   C. The fate of the hostile heathen. 14:12-15
   D. The universal worship of Jehovah. 14:16-21

Comments

Beginning with the ninth chapter we enter upon an entirely new section of the book, one which few if any scholars regard as having been written by the author of the first section. For comments on these chapters the student is referred to the Bible dictionary and the commentary. The outline above is from *The Abingdon Bible Commentary.** It presents a point of view worthy of consideration along with that presented by the Westminster Bible dictionary and Dummelow's commentary.

MALACHI—THE PROPHET OF JUDGMENT AND MERCY

Outline

I. GOD'S LOVE; ISRAEL'S INGRATITUDE. 1:1—2:16
   A. Choice of Jacob instead of Esau. 1:1-5
   B. A rebuke of the priests. 1:6-14
      1. Their sacrifices were unacceptable because they had lost the spirit of worship.

---

* Edited by Frederick Carl Eiselen, Edwin Lewis, and David G. Downey. Used by permission of the publishers, Abingdon-Cokesbury Press.

2. Even among the Gentiles there is pure worship of Jehovah.
C. The priests are warned of punishment. 2:1-9
   1. Instead of authority they would be subjected to insults. 2:1-4
   2. An ideal priest described. 2:5-7
   3. The covenant corrupted. 2:8-9
D. The people are guilty of estrangement from God. 2:10-16
   1. Have sinned in marrying those with strange gods. 2:10-11
   2. The resulting punishment. 2:12-13
   3. The evil of divorce—a sin against "the wife of thy youth." 2:14-16

II. FAITHLESSNESS EXPOSED AND REBUKED. 2:17—3:6
   A. The age-old attempt to justify one's behavior. 2:17
   B. A messenger sent to execute God's justice. 3:1-6
      1. Upon the sons of Levi (priest). 3:3
      2. Upon the people. 3:5-6

III. CALL TO REPENTANCE—REFLECTING CLEARLY A GOD OF JUDGMENT AND MERCY. 3:7—4:6
   A. A rebuke and a command with promise. 3:7-12
   B. The doubters and their response. 3:13-18
      1. Confusion revealed. 3:13-15
      2. A new discernment. 3:16-18
   C. God's justice distinguishes between the righteous and the wicked. 4:1-3
   D. Concluding appeal and promise. 4:4-6

Comments

It will be of interest to the reader to know that there are those who think Malachi simply means "my messenger" and is not the name of the writer of the prophecy which is popularly ascribed to one whose name is Malachi. While the exact date is uncertain there are evidences that it was written between 460 and 445 B.C., probably about the time of the work of Ezra and Nehemiah in Jerusalem. There are those who think that it may have been written as late as 420 B.C.

The book itself indicates that the revival of religious interest stirred up by the preaching of Haggai and Zechariah had died away and that the spiritual state of the people had become distressing. It may be that the writer of this book knew of the revival under the preaching of his predecessors and is reflecting some of his own pessimism because of the people's lapse.

The style is quite different from that of the other writers. The argumentative method is employed all the way through. The first and second chapters indicate that the religious observances had been greatly affected, as evidenced by the loss of a spirit of worship. The priests are threatened because of their failure to be true, sincere, and diligent in the discharge of their duties.

With an ineffective priesthood it is not surprising to discover that Judah had become estranged from her God and had made unholy alliances with peoples of other religions. Here her relationship to God is likened to family disharmony so prevalent when the prophecy was written. This particular emphasis is very much like that of Nehemiah, who came to Jerusalem about this time. The student who wishes a clear understanding of the religious, political, and social situation in Palestine will do well to study the books of Ezra and Nehemiah at this point. The bitter attack of Nehemiah upon the evils of divorce, and his insistence that the Jews who had married Gentiles be separated from them, had more significance than may be noted by a casual reading of the account. The intermarriage with other peoples was resulting in the introduction of other religious practices and as such was greatly weakening Jewish faith in the one true God.

The age-old attempt to justify one's behavior is forcefully stated in the last verse of the second chapter. The "My Messenger" of the first verse of the third chapter (from which the name of the book probably comes) was sent to execute God's justice. It will be noticed that in this the priests and the people are specifically pointed out as the objects of God's disfavor.

The appeal for Israel to return is probably another way of calling on her to repent. Here the appeal is stated in an argumentative style. A careful study of the responses of men and women who are reluctant to submit to the demands of religion may reveal that subjectively we are raising just such questions as the people of Malachi's day asked. Chapter 3, verses 7-12, is one of the favorite passages of those who preach on the subject of stewardship. It raises a problem by apparently equating blessings with material prosperity, for there are certainly many blessings far superior to material wealth.

The fourth chapter reveals the magnificent conception of God as just and merciful. He distinguishes between the righteousness and the wicked, which is an expression of justice. His mercy is beautifully expressed in the closing verse: "Behold, I will send you Elijah the prophet before the great and terrible day of the LORD come. And he shall turn the heart of the fathers to the children, and the heart of the children to their fathers; lest I come and smite the earth with a curse."

*   *   *   *   *

Your study of the minor prophets has revealed that the order in which they are arranged in the Bible is not chronological. It is probable that some were written later than Malachi. We have, however, come to the end of the study of them as they appear in the Bible. Throughout these books attention is directed to the fact that the relationship of the people to God has been far from satisfactory. The lights and shadows have played alternately upon that relationship, but all the way through there has been one continuing note— the survival of the remnant and the ultimate realization of God's will and purpose as expressed in his covenant with Abraham.